The CALVIN INSTITUTE OF CHRISTIᴌ
STUDIES Series, edited by John D. Witvlie͚ ͟.ͅ.ͦ.ͭ.ͤ reflection on the history, theology, and practice of Christian worship
and to stimulate worship renewal in Christian congregations. Contributions include writings by pastoral worship leaders from a wide
range of communities and scholars from a wide range of disciplines.
The ultimate goal of these contributions is to nurture worship practices that are spiritually vital and theologically rooted.

Published

We Have Seen His Glory

A VISION OF KINGDOM WORSHIP

Ben Witherington III

[handwritten annotations:]

p. 31 value added plus sign.

1 + 1 + 1 = 3 Man adds

1 × 1 × 1 = 1 God multiplies

p. 72 doxology

William B. Eerdmans Publishing Company

Grand Rapids, Michigan / Cambridge, U.K.

© 2010 Ben Witherington III
All rights reserved

Published 2010 by
Wm. B. Eerdmans Publishing Co.
2140 Oak Industrial Drive N.E., Grand Rapids, Michigan 49505 /
P.O. Box 163, Cambridge CB3 9PU U.K.
www.eerdmans.com

Printed in the United States of America

16 15 14 13 12 11 10   7 6 5 4 3 2 1

Library of Congress Cataloging-in-Publication Data

Witherington, Ben, 1951-
    We have seen His glory: a vision of kingdom worship /
    Ben Witherington III.
          p.   cm. — (The Calvin Institute of Christian Worship
          liturgical studies series)
    ISBN 978-0-8028-6528-1 (pbk.: alk. paper)
    1. Public worship.   I. Title.

BV15.W58   2010
264 — dc22

                                        2009044733

For President Tim Tennent and Julie Tennent.

We are so glad you have graced us with
your presence here at Ashbury!

Contents

Prelude

One of the things that has preoccupied my mind in recent years is the issue of worship. I have been surprised to discover how very little time New Testament scholars spend talking about it, or even about the texts in the Bible that describe worship. I have looked in vain for good textbooks written by biblical scholars on what the Bible, or even just the New Testament, says about worship.[1] As Shakespeare would say, this is "passing strange," especially since worship is something most of us are involved in every single week. Perhaps one reason for this surprising silence comes to light when I report a recent discussion I had with a New Testament colleague.

I asked him where he was going to church these days. He beat around the bush for a while, then confessed that he hadn't yet come upon a church that he and his wife really found "ministered to them" and got them excited about worshipping God. So they went to church sporadically and tried different churches, never

---

1. For example, hardly a passing reference is made to a theology of worship in the otherwise useful recent study *Theological Interpretation of the New Testament,* ed. Kevin Vanhoozer (Grand Rapids: Baker, 2005), and even Frank Matera's full dress and very helpful study *New Testament Theology* (Louisville: Westminster/John Knox, 2007) gives scant attention to the subject. The Old Testament was covered long ago by H. H. Rowley, but his study is very dated at this juncture.

committing to one in particular. These were revealing comments, and what they revealed is that my friend had gotten caught up in the consumer approach to worship, the attitude that one goes to a church because it "ministers to me." Not, mind you, "I go to a church because that's where I can best serve" but rather "I go to a church where I am best served." This sort of anthropocentric or consumer-oriented approach to worship is all too common in our narcissistic culture, and it got me thinking about what the New Testament actually says about worship, especially about the ultimate and final vision of worship, both heavenly and eschatological worship as depicted, for example, in the book of Revelation. Alas, worship as we experience it is imperfect, always caught betwixt and between, but perhaps a clearer vision of what worship can be will give us some guidance for better praxis of the art of worshipping.

My thoughts on this subject have developed over time. I have been an academic for the last thirty years and also have served as pastor of six churches along the way. Some urgency came into my thinking when I realized how little theological reflection goes into the planning of a worship service these days. Whether the service is some form of "traditional" worship or a modern "praise" service, whether it is highly liturgical or just a "hymn sandwich," worship as we practice it seems to dwell entirely too much on the past and too little on the finish line — the Kingdom Come. Suppose, however, we were to "play it forward" rather than replaying it backward? Suppose we envisioned Christian worship in light of the eschaton rather than in light of what has already gone before in the past, in light of Kingdom Come rather than in light of kingdoms gone? And trust me, in America there are some ecclesiastical kingdoms which have come and gone, even though some Christians are fervently praying that next year will be 1954. In this little study I hope to explore the possibilities of a Kingdom Come sort of worship. What would that look like, and could we get excited about it and actually do it? Isn't it about time, in the early years of the twenty-first century, that we thought seriously and theologically about these matters?

I am convinced that one of the great deterrents to having a more reflective and more Christian approach to worship is that even many of our ministers and worship leaders have very little understanding of what the New Testament actually says about worship — what it is meant to be, what it entails, and what we ought to do. In this study I hope to offer certain remedies to that problem and tease some minds into active thought about what worship should look like if we really believe that God's Kingdom is coming. In so doing I hope to make clear that worship should involve "an assurance of things hoped for, and a conviction about things not yet seen" (Heb. 11:1), and so should be an act of forward-looking faith, hope, and love.

I hope that these opening remarks have piqued your curiosity. Now it's time for us to explore a more biblical and Kingdom-oriented vision of worship.[2]

Easter 2009

---

2. I have already written three volumes on the sacraments (published by Baylor University Press in 2006 and 2007): one on baptism *(Troubled Waters)*, one on the Lord's Supper *(Making a Meal of It)*, and one on the Word of God as sacramental *(The Living Word of God)*. Accordingly, I do not intend to focus on those aspects of worship in this particular study, not because I don't think they're an important part of worship — I absolutely do. Rather, I want to focus more broadly on a proper theological understanding of and orientation to what Christian worship actually is and does.

CHAPTER ONE

We Have Seen His Glory:
The Day Is Coming and Now Is

It must be a gift of evolution that humans
Can't sustain wonder. We'd never have gotten up
From our knees if we could.

Robert Hass, *Time and Materials: Poems, 1997-2005*

If there is one characteristic more than others that contempo-
rary public worship needs to recapture, it is this awe before the
surpassingly great and gracious God.

Henry Sloane Coffin

The story in John 4 of Jesus and the Samaritan woman at the well
is one of the most beloved and belabored of all Gospel tales. While
on the surface it may seem a rather pastoral or idyllic tale, it is in
fact one fraught with social tension, and we will be well served to
consider it in some depth before we inquire about its importance
for our discussion of worship.

As most readers of this study will already know, the animus
between Jews and Samaritans was enormous at this point in history, and from the outset this fact is underlined by two statements
— Jesus leaves Judea and "*has* to go through Samaria" (John 4:4,

emphasis mine) in order to get to Galilee, presumably because he wants to get to Galilee quickly. What is implied is that he might have preferred the more roundabout way, or at least his disciples might have preferred it; many Jews took it to avoid Samaritan territory. Verse 9 further underlines the fractured nature of the relationship between Jews and Samaritans. When Jesus asks the woman at the well for a drink of water, the Evangelist tells us that "Jews do not share things in common with Samaritans." More broadly, we could say that *even in a setting where hospitality was supposed to be universally offered, Jews and Samaritans disliked each other so much, they were totally inhospitable toward each other.* This explains quite clearly the reaction of the Samaritan woman to Jesus' request. Jews and Samaritans wouldn't eat or drink together, wouldn't work together, and most certainly wouldn't worship together.

The social setting of the discussion between Jesus and the Samaritan woman is also crucial to understanding the tale, because it is not just anywhere in Samaria that Jesus chooses to ask for water — it is at Jacob's well near Sychar, one of the great holy places for Samaritans, who affirmed only the patriarchal religion of the Pentateuch, the religion of Abraham, Isaac, and Jacob. For Samaritans, worship focused on the theology of the Pentateuch, the worship practices mentioned in the Pentateuch and known to be practiced by the patriarchs, and on Mt. Gerizim. Samaritans were not interested in worship patterns that didn't exist before David and Solomon, who aren't mentioned in the Pentateuch, or in Temple-focused worship in Jerusalem, which was the legacy of those monarchs.

One further feature, an anomaly, sets up the story. Jesus is tired and sits by the well at midday, which is not at all the normal hour for a woman to come and draw water. This signals something is awry. (Further, Jesus' making his request of a woman he doesn't know is in part precipitated by the fact that his disciples have gone to town to buy food and are not available to help him.)

We Have Seen His Glory

It is interesting that the woman instantly knows that Jesus isn't a Samaritan (v. 9). Is it because of his accent, or because she's accustomed to Pentateuchal Hebrew, and he speaks to her in Aramaic? We cannot be sure. In any case, the great divide between them is punctuated from the outset. The woman's question is direct: "How can you, a Jew, ask me, a Samaritan woman, for a drink?" This violated several possible protocols: Jewish men weren't supposed to speak to strange women; Jews weren't supposed to speak to Samaritans; and men weren't supposed to speak to immoral women (for we later learn that the Samaritan woman is such). Jesus shouldn't have spoken to this woman at all, much less asked for a cup of water which she had touched and so made unclean. But Jesus is unconcerned with such rules. He is simply thirsty. Or is something else really going on here? *meaning or intent*

Verse 10 suggests that the main issue is not Jesus' needing a favor, but the woman's needing to ask Jesus for "living water," a typical Johannine double entendre which in its mundane sense means "running water" (i.e., a stream). Notice as well that Jesus suggests that the woman is ignorant of "the gift of God." What does this connote? It doesn't seem to mean the same thing as "the generosity of God," or Jesus would have said so. Is Jesus saying, "If you knew me, the gift of God, and so knew who was asking you for water . . ."? This is possible. What both the context and the opening character of this dialogue do is set up the obviously theological discussion that ensues, which highlights the difference between Jesus' worship theology and traditional Samaritan worship theology, which is Pentateuchally based, land-locked, holy place–centered, and not at all Davidically messianic in character.

The dialogue takes an interesting turn at verse 12, where the woman, apparently exasperated with Jesus because he seems to actually have nothing to offer her but verbiage, says, "Are you greater than our father Jacob, who gave us this well . . . ?" Jesus' immediate reply implies that the answer to this question is yes. Jacob left only ordinary water for the Samaritans, though that was a most precious gift in a dry and weary land. But Jesus is offering an everlasting and deeply spiritual source of refreshment which will quench souls' thirst once and for all. Indeed, Jesus says he offers water that, when imbibed, "will become in them a spring of water welling up to everlasting life" — in short, the gift that keeps on giving. Jesus would seem to be referring to the gift of the Holy Spirit, for later Paul, perhaps reflecting on this very saying, remarks, "for we were all baptized by one Spirit into one body, whether Jews or Greeks, slaves or free, *and we were all given the one Spirit to drink*" (1 Cor. 12:13, emphasis mine).

Alas, as verse 15 shows, the woman still doesn't get the spiritual point and asks for directions to the stream nearer town so that she doesn't have to continue to make such trips to the well in the heat of the day, and especially can avoid the scrutiny of her fellow Samaritans (and in particular the women who draw water early in the morning). And it is at this juncture in the dialogue that Jesus chooses to puncture the woman's façade. "Go and call your husband and come back," he urges, to which she abruptly replies, "I have no husband!" Jesus then proceeds to tell her that technically she is correct, since she has had five husbands and the man she now lives with is not her husband. It is this word of prophetic insight into the actual condition of the woman's life and her past that causes her façade to crumble, and a real theological dialogue to ensue.

But then the woman makes a foray into flattery: "I perceive you are a prophet, sir" (surely the highest compliment a Samaritan could give, since Samaritans believed that the messianic figure would be a prophet after the manner of Moses). Is this, and her tandem foray into theological speculation about the best holy mountain, an artful dodge? Like so many before her and since, is she holding the personal ethical questions at bay by offering instead to debate worship theology? Perhaps. In any case, Jesus takes the bait to debate and declares outright, "Believe me, woman, a time is coming when you will worship the Father neither on this mountain nor in Jerusalem. You Samaritans worship what you do not know; we worship what we do know, for salvation is from the Jews. Yet a time is coming and has now come when the true worshippers will worship the Father in spirit and truth, for they are the kind of worshippers the Father seeks. God is spirit, and his worshippers must worship in spirit and truth" (vv. 21-24).

This is one of the most intriguing segments of continuous theological reflection in this entire Gospel, and we must give it due attention, but note that the woman's response and confession — "I know that Messiah is coming. . . . When he comes, he will proclaim all things to us" — is true enough but inadequate. Jesus in turn replies, "I am he, the one who is speaking to you." Jesus will deal with the woman where she is in her intellectual, spiritual, and ethical pilgrimage, and he will seek to lead her beyond it. Interestingly, the woman says no more, abandons her water jar, and runs back to town, both confessing that she has been unmasked and wondering out loud if Jesus could be the Redeemer longed for by the Samaritans and predicted by Moses.

Let us return for a moment to Jesus' words in verses 21-24. Is verse 21 a warning about the Jewish war that was to come in the sixties and ruin temple-centered religion, especially in Jerusalem, but also cause trouble in Samaria? This may well be so. Verse 22 is even more intriguing. Jesus seems to suggest that the Samaritans are worshipping the true God, but doing so in ignorance. He then asserts that Jews know *whom* they worship because "salvation is from the Jews," by which Jesus seems to mean that the revelation of the true identity and nature of God came to the Jews, and therefore they have the saving knowledge of God which the Samaritans lack. But the Samaritans had the Pentateuch — did Jesus see that as inadequate? Apparently so, as did most Jews. The Prophets and even the Writings were crucial to knowing God and the full revelation of the divine nature and salvation.

This comports quite well with the constant theme of this Gospel, for we have a crescendo of confessions in this book, all of which are true but inadequate until we arrive at the Easter confession of Thomas in John 20. Verse 23, however, adds more fuel to the fire. Jesus speaks of a time which has *already begun* when the true worshippers of the one true God will worship in spirit and truth, the very kind of worshippers God seeks. But what does this mean?

Should we be capitalizing the word *Spirit* here? I think we probably should, not least because of the close association of Spirit and truth, and because the Spirit is the one who leads the disciple into all truth in John 14–17. In other words, Jesus is announcing that the time for eschatological worship is dawning, worship grounded in a clear knowledge of the truth/revelation and salvation that has come from the Jews in the person of Jesus, and is guided and inspired by the indwelling presence of the Holy Spirit.

Why is it that God wants that sort of worshipper? Apparently because it comports with the very nature of God — who is Spirit and who is The Truth — and so his true worshippers need to be offering worship that involves both the truth and the Spirit, not ignorance and the absence of the Spirit. Yet, Jesus did imply that the Samaritans were worshipping the true God in ignorance, it would seem. We could say a good deal about the rest of this story,[1] but it doesn't bear on our discussion of worship and the points we need now to highlight:

1. Jesus says *the time is now* for the beginning of a kind of worship that is eschatological in character, and dwells no more on the old culture wars, the worship wars, the edifice complex, the "in which building is true worship happening" issue. Worship in spirit and truth can happen anywhere and everywhere, and one does not need to go on pilgrimage to Jerusa-

1. On which see Witherington, *The Indelible Image*, vol. 2 (Downers Grove, Ill.: InterVarsity Press, 2009).

lem or anywhere else to find it. Why is that? Because, of course, through the Christ event, the Spirit is made universally available. God's presence is not a "located" presence, nor should it even be conceived of as a located presence anymore, as if God dwells in buildings made by human hands.

2. True worship comes from the same source as genuine salvation, which is to say that it comes from the same source as living water — God, in the person of his Son, Jesus. Jesus says that Jews know whom they worship, which is an essential prerequisite to being saved, and thus to offering true worship in spirit and truth. True worship is a result of having a saving relationship with God. Indeed, as we will have many occasions to say in this study, worship is the ultimate aim and goal of salvation. Salvation is but a means to an end, not an end in itself.

3. The character of the worship should comport with the character of the one being worshipped — the one true God who is spirit.

The story in John 4 is remarkably rich, both theologically and ethically, but here it will be wise to emphasize the ethical point that believing in Jesus is seen as an ethical act, the *right* thing to do. Furthermore, we are reminded that the Gospel breaks down ethnic barriers in such a fashion that even Samaritans can be saved, for while salvation is from the Jews, it is for the world, and Jesus is the Savior of the world. Neither immorality nor gender difference nor ethnicity nor varied religious praxis prove to be barriers that Jesus and the Gospel cannot hurdle on the road to a worldwide people of God.

Equally important, here is where I stress that true worship is an ethical act. Indeed, it is the fulfillment of the Great Commandment to love God with all our being, and also the fulfillment of those mandates from the Ten Commandments to have no other gods and make no idols. Let me say that again: *Worship is the ulti-*

mate ethical act on earth, the most important act on earth because it is the ultimate fulfillment of the Shema, the Great Commandment, and indeed the First and Second Commandments.

But there is a hint of something more here which has to do with things eschatological. Listen again to Jesus' words from John 4 in a more literal translation: "But the hour is coming and now is when the true/genuine worshippers will worship the Father in spirit and in truth, for the Father is seeking these sorts of worshippers. God is spirit, and for those [truly] worshipping him, it is a necessity to worship him in spirit and in truth."

This, I submit, is an eschatological manifesto, a throwing down of the gauntlet. Worship can no longer be just the same old thing. Jesus is inaugurating, without fully explaining, eschatological worship, and he tells us that worshippers who worship in spirit and truth are the very sort of worshippers whom God is seeking. In fact, Jesus insists that it is necessary to worship God in spirit and truth, now that he has come and brought in the Kingdom on earth.

To fully grasp the import of this, we must remember the social context. Worship of Jews and Samaritans was ethnocentric and patrilocal. It was temple-centered and priest-controlled. It focused on literal sacrifices, and it was a smelly, noisy, messy process. Jesus is inaugurating a worship without temples, priests, and literal sacrifices, all of which are said to be fulfilled by and in Jesus. He is the new temple of God, where God's presence dwells (see John 2). He is the Passover lamb who takes away the sins of the world (see John 1). And he is the priest who will offer himself as the perfect sacrifice in Jerusalem on Golgotha's heights, a theology spelled out in great detail in the book of Hebrews.

Henceforth, now that the eschatological age has begun, true worshippers will not be needing the old sorts of temples located in particular "high holy places"; will not be needing the old sorts of sacrifices, since Christ's sacrifice will make literal sacrifices both fulfilled and obsolete; will not be needing the old sorts of priests as human mediators between God and humanity. In the new covenant which "now is," the only priests are Christ, the heavenly high priest, and the priesthood of all believers. The only sacrifices are of self, of service, of true praise and worship. And the only temples are the Body of Christ collectively (i.e., the church), and one's own physical body, for that is where God in Christ now dwells.

Eschatological worship dwells no more in the past. It is forward-looking and forward-thinking, and it focuses on the future and what it means to worship in spirit and truth, rather than in Swansea and Duluth. God is eagerly seeking such worship and such worshippers. The only question is, Can we handle it? When the writer of the Gospel of John says, "we have seen his glory," he probably means that he has seen the radiant risen Christ, the Christ who began the new age in earnest on Easter, though even before then there were harbingers of it. And when we have seen the vision glorious, there is only one fully adequate response: to glorify God with all that we have and all that we are. In the next chapter we will consider another Johannine text which helps us to think further about these things: Revelation 4–5.

Questions for Reflection and Discussion

1. What do you think the phrase "worship in Spirit and truth" really involves? Is this about the substance of worship? One's approach to worship? The style of worship? Or all three?

2. One of the major emphases in this chapter is that worship is a supremely ethical act. In fact, I emphasized the point that worship is the ultimate ethical act on earth, the most important act on earth because it is the ultimate fulfillment of the Shema, the Great Commandment — and, indeed, of the First and Second Commandments. Do you agree with this assessment? If so, how do you think it should orient your priorities?

3. Worship often tends to have very specific cultural forms of expression. But Jesus seems to have been talking about a kind of worship which recognizes that the Kingdom is breaking into human history, and it transcends and indeed transforms cultural stereotypes, particularly about the necessity of worshipping in specific sacred places. What implications do you think this has for our theology of sacred structures, of church buildings?

4. Why do you think the ancients considered mountains or high places to be especially appropriate places for acts of worship? What do you think Jesus thought of such a theology?

CHAPTER TWO

Glorifying the Creator and Redeemer: Revelation 4–5

> *To great sections of the Church the art of worship has been lost entirely, and in its place has come that strange and foreign thing called the "program." This word has been borrowed from the stage and applied with sad wisdom to the type of public service which now passes for worship among us.*
>
> A. W. Tozer, *The Pursuit of God*

> *Worship changes the worshiper into the image of the One worshiped.*
>
> Jack Hayford

Glory Hallelujah

Of late there have been some odd *theologia gloriae* on offer in the conservative Protestant world. The language of glory is, of course, a rich and varied one in the Bible. Sometimes it simply refers to God's radiance, or just his bright presence, or more generally the divine presence. Sometimes it refers to God vindicating his character or name or plan (which is what the phrase "glorify your name" would normally mean in a text like John 12:28). Sometimes we hear about the Father glorifying the Son or vice versa, which is an interpersonal act, not a self-referential one (see John 17:4-5). We also hear about the Son giving his glory (read "presence") to his disciples so that they may be one (John 17:22). Apparently glory is something that God and Christ are perfectly willing to share with human beings, particularly their followers. Sometimes "glory" refers to the effect of that divine presence when God makes his imprint on his people and they not only see God's glory but begin to be transfixed and transfigured into God's likeness, or, as Paul puts it, they are conformed to the image of God's glorious Son, or, as the author of 2 Peter 1 puts it, they become partakers of the divine nature. Second Corinthians 3 talks about our transformation in these terms, and I will say more about that shortly.

But sometimes, when the subject of glory comes up, some theologians suggest that God is all about seeking his own glory. Rather than being seen as a glory-giver, God in essence is viewed as a glory-grabber deeply worried if he doesn't get enough credit.[1] In other words, God is ultimately a self-centered being in earnest about glorifying himself. Even God's saving people is viewed ultimately as serving the purpose of expanding God's fan club.

I must say that I find this whole approach to the biblical discussion of glory very wide of the mark, if it is true that Jesus Christ is the perfect revelation of what God's character is like. Perhaps you will remember the language of Hebrews 1, which says that Christ is the effulgence, the very beaming out of God's glory. Christ himself, it will be remembered, said that he came, trailing clouds of glory, perhaps, but not to be served but to serve others and to give his life as a ransom for the many (Mark 10:45). This does not sound like self-glorification to me. It sounds like self-sacrificial love. And if the Son is indeed the spitting image of the Father, and if God's enduring and endearing character is indeed

---

1. Honestly, it is hard for me to imagine God in the image of a narcissistic sports figure.

love (as 1 John says), then I doubt that narcissism is the ultimate character trait of God. However, our present concern is not with what God does with glory, but with the glorifying that we as human beings are supposed to do, for it is indeed our task to glorify God and love God forever. That is in essence what worship is about. I have written a sermon on the subject which will help us get into the subject more directly, and we shall turn to it now.

Sermon: Transfigured

Isaiah's Vision

It happened to Isaiah a long time ago. He went into the Temple and encountered more than he had counted on. He says, "I saw the Lord . . ." (Isa. 6:1). The Temple was seen as the juncture between earth and heaven, and he had a close encounter of the first kind with the Almighty. The thing about any such encounter, if it really is God one is encountering, is that it is a matter of communion between two beings of very different orders. A close encounter with God, paradoxically enough, both widens and narrows the gap between us and God. It *widens* it because any such genuine encounter makes clear that God is God and we are not! Notice what Isaiah says: "Woe unto me! I am a man of unclean lips" (Isa. 6:5). God is the Holy One, and Isaiah, even with his priestly and prophetic pedigree, is most definitely *not* the Holy One. Worship happens when the creature realizes he is not the Creator, and bows down before and adores the one who is. That is true worship. It is about giving up, surrendering, presenting yourself as a living sacrifice, bowing down, recognizing, and restoring the creation order of things.

But encountering God also *narrows* the gap between us in the sense that when we bow down, God condescends to come down to our level and honors our worship, and we encounter God. Worship creates a communion which maintains the separation of God and humankind. At the same time, if worship is carried out meaningfully, it draws humankind toward God and away from the self-centered love that is ultimately so unsatisfying. G. K. Chesterton once said, "A man may be said loosely to love himself, but he can hardly fall in love with himself, or, if he does, it must be a monotonous courtship."

Worship is not about our cozying up to God, our buddy or pal. There is, of course, intimacy with *Abba*, but we are in no way being set up in a partnership of equals in worship. A partnership or *koinonia* between equals results in fellowship, not worship. So let us be clear: the experience of Isaiah was worship. Any experience which seeks to put us up on God's level is not worship. It is inappropriate and even shocking familiarity; indeed, it can even be called idolatry. God condescends and remains God; we do not ascend and become as gods. If we once ceased to be creatures and became absorbed by the deity, we would no longer be capable of worship. Worship inherently implies a distinction between the worshipper and the one worshipped. Furthermore, when real worship happens, we become even more creaturely, even more of what we were intended to be as images of God. We become eternal worshippers of the Triune One.

The English word *worship* actually comes from the combination of two words, *worth* and *ship* from Old English. It has to do with honoring, giving homage to one who is worthy to receive such praise, attention, obeisance — "Thou art worthy." We, by contrast, are not worthy of such absolute, unconditional devotion and adoration. Idolatry is the polar opposite of true worship. It is ascribing deity to, and serving and sublimating one's self before, something that is less than God Almighty — a human ruler, a parent, a friend, a conquerer, a lover, a teacher or mentor, or even one's self. There are many forms that idolatry can take. When you make another human being your object of ultimate concern and unquestioned love, you in fact have committed a form of idolatry. And however good your relationship is with that "significant other," it is no substitute for one's relationship with God, and for worshipping the one true God.

Ezekiel's Experience

But consider another Old Testament worship experience. Just like Isaiah, Ezekiel was taken by surprise by God, "the Hound of Heaven" who just keeps coming our way in divine condescension, even in surprising places. Isaiah had his close encounter and was transfigured in the Temple. But Ezekiel was in exile in Babylon, sitting by the Chebar canal swatting mosquitoes the size of small birds, when God gave him the awesome throne-chariot vision. For Ezekiel, worship was not a matter of being in a holy place. Rather, he learned that the earth is the Lord's and the fullness thereof — even in the Land of the Exile. God's presence can be encountered anywhere, at any time.

This vision was crucial not only for Ezekiel, but also for John of Patmos, who saw the throne-chariot vision in a modified form. To be sure, John, like Ezekiel, was not in a church or a synagogue when he saw the *mysterium tremendum* recorded in Revelation 4. He too was in exile, on a rock pile off the coast of Asia Minor (modern Turkey), when he said, "I was in the Spirit on the Lord's day, and I heard . . . and I saw . . ." (Rev. 1:10-13). He was in the Spirit, not in the church. Worship is not a matter of holy space; it's a matter of a holy, or at least receptive, condition. And the mention of the Lord's Day may suggest a holy time, a time for worship. It is no accident that Ezekiel had his vision on the very day that he should have been anointed priest in the Temple in Jerusalem. It was a holy time for him.

Caught Up in the Spirit, Caught Up in Worship

Our proper text for today, Revelation 4, raises compelling questions about the nature of worship and our posture and preparation for it. So often we will hear people say, "I don't go to that worship service because I don't get anything out of it." But wait a minute — Who is supposed to be doing the worshipping here? If it is the congregant, then the primary question should be "Where can I go to best *give* praise and worship to God?" not "Where can I go to *get* the most out of it?"

 There was an elderly woman in my home church who could barely see or hear. Yet there she was each Sunday, sitting near the front and participating in worship with vigor. At one point, a young woman asked her why she was there, since she couldn't really hear much of what was being said or see much of what was happening. Her reply was memorable: "I'm not here for what I can get out of the service but for what I can give. I get the bulletin mailed to me, and I get out my magnifying glass and read it through, and then I read the Scriptures and the hymns we will sing. I think and pray through what may be God's Word for me in this. So when I come to the service, I'm ready to worship, and I give that to God, even though I'm getting back perhaps less than some in that particular hour." The young woman was stunned. Caught up in the consumer mentality of many, and applying it to worship, she had just assumed that one chose a worship service — or, for that matter, a church — based on what one could get out of it, not on where God might be best pleased to receive our worship and service.

Worship is not and never was intended to be a spectator sport or the performance of the few for the benefit of the many couch potatoes in the pew. The consumer approach to worship puts the emphasis almost entirely on the wrong syllable. It leads to pastors desperately seeking to change acts of worship and worship patterns in an attempt to attract a bigger crowd, the theory being that worship should be a matter of giving the people what they want and crave. This is completely wrong. Worship is a matter of giving to God what he desires and requires of us. If you end up with a nice "buzz" because of it, that's a bonus and a by-product; it's not what worship is striving for. Remember that John of Patmos was not looking for a more *au courant* worship service when he was in the Spirit on the Lord's Day and received a vision.

Consider first the prerequisite for John's receiving the vision. It was not that the right mood was being set by the music. (The function of music in worship is not to set the mood or even to rev up the troops, but rather to engage them at the affective level so that their whole beings — body, mind, emotions, will, spirit — are caught up in wonder, love, and praise of God.) It was not that John was in the right place. It was rather that he came prepared for an encounter in holy time; he came prepared to give honor and praise and glory on the Lord's Day. He was wide open to the Spirit to such a degree that the text says he was in the Spirit. Notice it does not say that the Spirit was in him, though that is also true. No, he had already immersed himself in the divine presence before the vision came. This likely means that he had prepared his heart to worship, he had repented of his sins, he had been shriven or cleansed, and so he boldly approached the Presence and immersed himself in God.

And when God gave him the vision, what a vision it was — one of heavenly worship that transfixed and transfigured him. He saw representatives of all the different orders of creatures lifting up God on God's throne: animals, humans, and angels were all symbolically present in the Presence of God, lifting up God on his throne. The twenty-four elders represent God's people, both old and new, and though they were given thrones, they fell down before him who was on the throne and worshipped him. The living creatures with eyes everywhere, seeing all there was to see, looked on in wide-eyed amazement and never stopped saying, "Holy, Holy, Holy is the Lord God the Almighty, now and forever" (Rev. 4:8).

The four living creatures — the human, the ox, the eagle, and the lion — are representative samplings from the four orders of all creation (and, interestingly enough, they became the four symbols for the four canonical Gospels). The rabbis interpreting Ezekiel 1 said that the lion was the king of beasts, the eagle the king of the birds of the air, the ox the king of beasts of burden, and the human the king of all creation, so that this is a vision of all orders of creation literally lifting up the throne of God and the Holy One — all creatures great and small worshipping God!

Worthwhile Worship

Why is God worthy of such worship? Because he is the Creator God who made all creatures for just such a purpose. John Knox once said, "It is the chief aim of humankind to love God and enjoy and adore him for ever." The most important act on earth is worship. It completes the intended life cycle of all creatures great and small. The chief end of humankind and human history is *not* the salvation of all persons. I will say that again: *Salvation is not the point and goal of human history.* That is but a means to the ultimate end, which is the proper worship of God by all creatures. It is, of course, true that were we to go on to Revelation 5, we would also learn that worship is intended to include and focus on not only the Creator God, but also the Redeemer God — namely, the Lamb who is at the same time the Lion of the tribe of Judah! But redemption is a means to the end of true worship, a worship where every knee shall bow and every tongue confess.

So, let's review what we have learned. First, true worship requires that we be in the Spirit at the appropriate time for worship (e.g., the Lord's Day). Second, this in turn implies that we come as true worshippers wide open to giving praise and glory to God, having already received the grace necessary to be able to do so, having put aside all distractions and the sin that so readily encumbers us. Only so are we prepared to receive what God will give: the proclamation of his truth and the comfort of his presence. Third, worship is chiefly what *we* do: we come to give honor and glory to the Worthy One. We come primarily to give rather than to get. But hear the good news: God *also* comes to give! God bows down as we bow down to God. God comes to relate to, empower, heal, save,

We Have Seen His Glory

and give vision to his people and proclaim his truth. And, fourth, the vision John received was of heavenly worship.

The chief aim of worship is that we be caught up in wonder, love, and praise of God, and thereby get a glimpse of the heavenly worship which happens when and as we are worshipping. In other words, we get a glimpse of what is happening above, which is also a vision of our destiny, when heaven comes down and glory fills our souls, and we become God's music, become God's true temple, become the bride, become the new Jerusalem that God's holy presence comes to inhabit for ever and ever, Immanuel. But that is a subject for a homily on another occasion. For now I leave you with a story.

In August 2001, at the end of a tour of two of the lands of the Bible, my intrepid group of pilgrims who had been sojourning for two weeks in Greece and Italy spent their last Sunday morning in the catacombs on the edge of the eternal city, Rome. We were about two hundred feet underground, and it had been arranged that we would worship in one of the niches where the saints had been buried for hundreds of years, though their caskets and coffins had long since been moved elsewhere, so that all that remained visible were the holes in the walls, going up some twenty feet on either side of the narrow, barrel-vaulted apse in which we stood. Yet there was a heavy sense that the saints were worshipping there with us, and we with them.

I preached on 2 Corinthians 4, and after that we all took holy communion together. Our guide was Georgio Abate, a nominal Catholic who had been deeply moved by the service, perhaps especially by the singing, and he asked if he too might share in the communion. We of course were delighted he would ask. All of us, our hearts full of praise after a long journey, had sung together "Venite Adoremus, Venite Adoremus, Dominum" ("O come let us adore him, O come let us adore him, Christ the Lord"). In that moment we were caught up in the Spirit, caught up in wonder, love, and praise, and worship happened. But it was not just the experience of true worship that made the moment unforgettable. It was that we had worshipped with the great company of heaven, and God had come down and inhabited our praise. That close encounter of the first kind, that interchange between God and our small company of pilgrims, had made the time a holy time, and the exchange a holy exchange. And because of that we were not merely transfixed — we were transfigured in some small way into God's likeness, and, paradoxically enough, in and by the same act we had affirmed our lack of divinity, our creaturely nature. This was, is, and always will be the essence of true worship.

What the Sermon Teaches Us

There is much to unpack in this sermon, but let's start with a few basics. First of all, worship is in essence about declaring the worth of God, about adoration and praise, about publicly directing love toward God. It has a *theocentric* focus. The focus is not on the minister, or whoever may be directing worship, or on the choir, but on God. One of the more disturbing trends in modern worship is its *anthropocentric* character and focus. Worship is supposed to be the time when we take our eyes off ourselves and our fellow human beings and focus on God. *Worship is not fellowship.* There is a time and a place for fellowship, and it is not during worship. *Koinonia* by definition is human beings sharing something with each other. Corporate worship is not essentially about interpersonal exchange between humans; it is about union and communion with God. Even the Scripture reading and preaching is about God addressing us. When it is done properly, it is not about the human proclaimer; it is about the proclamation. All the obvious parts of worship — prayer, praise, confession, almsgiving, singing, reciting creeds or liturgy — are very clearly directed toward God.

What has happened to much of worship in Protestant America? As a real theology of worship has slipped away and, indeed, seldom been taught, Protestant worship has increasingly modeled itself on some form of entertainment — the performance of the few for the appreciation of the many listeners. And the performers begin to think that they're "performing" for the praise of the minister and the congregation, and of course the congregation begins to see itself as an audience, and, not surprisingly, what we end up with is applause, the glorification of human beings and their performance. But in worship, no one but God should be praised and glorified. "To God be the glory/great things he hath done . . ." should be the character and focus of any truly Christian worship service.

Second, we should take note of all three of the worship scenes I alluded to: Isaiah 6, Ezekiel 1, and Revelation 4–5. Notice that in each case we are told that the prophetic figure had a vision which prompted a worshipful response. All too often when people come to worship today, they do not come prepared for worship. They are not prepared to hear "Be still and know that I am God." They are hurried, harried, distracted, frazzled, annoyed, and in general not prepared to receive any kind of vision, and the result is that they are not prepared to commune with God. They're just hoping to learn something, perhaps, to take a little McNugget away from the sermon, or to enjoy a hymn or a song or two, and then leave. They can hardly say, as John did, "I was in the Spirit on the Lord's day, and I heard . . . and I saw . . ." A vision of worship comes to those who are in the Spirit at the time for worship, and before they speak or respond, they first encounter God by intently listening and looking. Have you seen the vision? Did you come to worship expecting one?

Now the thing about a vision is that it is God-initiated. It's not a matter of the choir revving up the congregation or the minister pumping up the crowd. It is about the anticipation of encounter, and the timely receptivity of worshippers to God's encountering them in worship, and then the appropriate glorifying in response.

It is true, of course, that worship is an imperfect art because it is something done by imperfect human beings. But if we believe that Christ's coming makes a difference and has made a difference in our lives, then Christian worship should look more like the heavenly and Kingdom-focused worship described in these visions and less like the *Stand-up Spotlight* on TV. It should involve all of those present. Did you notice that everyone in the throne room of God in Revelation 4 was worshipping — angels, human beings, the living creatures? Worship is what all creatures great and small were and are intended for. It does indeed complete the life cycle of each one of us, and it thus behooves us to do it well, and do it often.

As I said at the beginning of the sermon, there is a paradoxical character to worship because while it certainly creates communion and union between God and his people, it also reminds us and reinforces the fact that God is God, and we are not. That is, it reinforces the very character and nature of the creation order — the basic distinction between who ought to be worshipped and who ought to do the worshipping. What is blurred all too often in modern worship is the radical distinction between God and humankind. When we spend much of a worship service praising one another and focusing on one another and glorifying each other, we are engaging in idolatry, whether or not we are aware of it. We may not be literally erecting a golden calf, but we might as well be. Worship is not the time or place for human self-glorification.

This last point was brought home to me quite vividly when I was studying that peculiar passage in 1 Corinthians 11:2-16, the one about the head coverings. Why in the world does Paul go through a long, convoluted argument about apparel — just to make it clear that it's fine for women to pray and prophesy in worship? As it turns out, there are good theological reasons for this little discourse, reasons having to do with whose glory should be visible in worship. Notice the use of the *doxa* language in this passage in verse 7 and verse 15. In verse 7 Paul says that a man is the image and glory of God, and so should not have his head covered, whereas woman is the glory of man and should have her head covered. In verse 15 we read that a woman's hair is her glory, and one further peculiarity is mentioned in verse 10 — that she should wear the head covering "because of the angels." The underlying theology here is that *only God's glory should show up in Christian worship; the glory of human beings should not.* I take the reference to the angels as alluding to the fact that angels were God's guardians of the creation order, and especially in worship the creation order is supposed to be truly and rightly manifest. Again, human glory is not supposed to show up in worship. Since the wife is the glory of the husband (here the language suggests that Paul is talking about husbands and wives in particular, though it has ramifications for men and women in general), and since her hair is her own glory, her head should be covered for both of these reasons, and thus only God's glory remains in worship.

In order to envision this, one also needs to consider the social setting of the meeting — probably the close quarters of the atrium and/or dining room of a home — and one needs to bear in mind that the meeting was at night, so there were many lamps hanging to light the event. Into this setting walks a woman whose hair is fashionably piled on top of her head, with jewels and other ornaments adorning it.[2] (This, by the way, is why we have the exhortation in 1 Timothy 2:8-15 about women not wearing such things in worship.) In that setting a woman with such a hairstyle would have been more than a little distracting. This would have promoted comments about the woman, and worship is not the time or the place for humans to draw attention to themselves or glorify themselves. Thus Paul says, in effect, "Wear a head covering so only God's glory is evident in worship."

Let's go back to 1 Corinthians 11:7 for a moment — man is the image and glory of God. Paul knows perfectly well that both man and woman are created in God's image according to Genesis 1, and he's not denying that, but I want to reflect for a moment on his saying that man is the glory of God. This is a very odd statement if it is true that God is all about self-glorification. God's

2. On all this, see Witherington, *Conflict and Community in Corinth* (Grand Rapids: Wm. B. Eerdmans, 1994).

glory would be one thing, and human beings' glory something else — the image of God, perhaps, but not God's own glory. And yet this is what Paul says. Perhaps God is not as concerned about guarding his glory as some suggest. Perhaps he is perfectly happy with sharing it; indeed, perhaps salvation is a reclamation project meant to restore the glory of human beings, to restore them in the image of God. Perhaps this is why Paul says that "all have sinned and fallen short of the glory of God" (Rom. 3:23). A more literal reading of that verse would be "all have sinned and are lacking/failing to reach the glory of God."

And herein lies a secret. Human beings most perfectly *are* the glory of God when they most perfectly reflect (and deflect) that glory, and that happens when they are best glorifying God in worship. God is in the process of the sanctifying and finally the glorifying of human beings in the sense of getting them fully conformed to the image of God's glorious son Jesus, a process completed when Jesus returns and raises the dead. In the meantime, the best thing we can do to move that process along is get caught up in wonder, love, and praise of our God, in glorifying God. Worship happens when we best manifest God's glory here and now by the act of glorifying God. Some concluding reflections on 2 Corinthians 3 will not be amiss here.

Second Corinthians 3:7–4:18 is a long, complex Pauline argument, and our concern is limited to what Paul says here about glory. It can be summed up as follows. First, Moses came down from Sinai with a good suntan — that is, he had encounters with the very living presence of God, and he came down reflecting that, so much so that he had to wear a veil over his face, because it was reflecting the very glory of God, and the Israelites couldn't take it. But this glory was a fading glory, like a fading suntan, and Paul wants to contrast it with a more lasting glory — namely, Christ's glory. Second, in 2 Corinthians 4:4, in a phrase strikingly similar to that of 1 Corinthians 11:7, Paul speaks of "the light of the gospel of the glory of Christ," who is the very image or likeness of God.

Unlike the glory of Moses, the glory of Christ was not and is not a fading one. It keeps on beaming. Third, 2 Corinthians 3:18 is the crucial verse. After contrasting the fading glory of the Mosaic ministry and the enduring glory of the ministry of the new covenant and of Christ, Paul says this: "But we all, with unveiled face, contemplating as in a mirror the glory of the Lord, are transformed into that same image from glory to glory, by the Spirit of the Lord." Yes, Christ is the very presence and manifestation of God on earth, his glory and his image on earth, and we, on a lesser scale, are supposed to be the same. But here Paul tells something of how that happens: when we behold the glory of the Lord with unveiled face (and undistracted attention), we are changed into the image of Christ, from glory to glory. I take it that Paul is talking about seeing the vision glorious, just as he did on Damascus Road, and just as we can in Christian worship, and what happens when we see the vision of the one we adore and love, and worship him, is that *we become what we admire.* As we glorify God, God, ever the giving self-sacrificial one, is conforming us to the image of his Son, and so "we are changed into that same image from glory to glory," which, Paul says in 2 Corinthians 3:17, sets us free — free from being self-centered, self-preoccupied, self-concerned, selfish, free from the heart turned in upon itself. Real worship can do that to us: we become self-forgetful and get caught up in wonder and love and praise of God. It is about giving up, surrendering, presenting our selves as a living sacrifice, bowing down, recognizing, and restoring the creation order of things. But at the same time, God condescends to inhabit our praises, and we are transformed, made more Christ-like, from glory to glory into that self-same image that Christ bore. Adoration is the means of our glorification. Glorifying God is the means of our transformation into Christ's image.

This discussion reminds me of a familiar hymn, which I'm taking the liberty of modifying slightly: "Turn your eyes upon Jesus, look full in his glorious face, and the things of this world will grow strangely dim, in the light of his wonder and grace." Maybe, just maybe, the reason why we are not more sanctified souls is that we are not truly worshipping, we are not truly catching the vision of the Lord in worship. Maybe it's time to change all that.

One more thing. Revelation 4 is a theocentric vision of worship, but Revelation 5 is a Christocentric one that focuses on the slain Lamb who yet lives and reigns from heaven. John intended to leave us with the understanding that Christian worship was meant to be Christocentric as a part of its theocentricity. It was not enough to recapitulate the experience of Ezekiel; Revelation 4 is a modification of that. No, one also needs to catch a glimpse of the Savior, the one who took away the sins of the world, the Passover lamb, who became the Risen One. Revelation 5 is a vision of all redemption, just as Revelation 4 is a vision of all creation. John's point is this: Revelation 5 brings to completion Revelation 4, and indeed, salvation is what makes possible John's having either of these visions. The question for us is this: Have we seen the vision of the Risen One? Do we know how to respond if we have caught the vision? Do we know the meaning of true worship in spirit and truth? We must explore these things more fully in the next chapter as we examine the differences between Old Testament and New Testament worship.

Questions for Reflection and Discussion

1. One of the questions raised at the beginning of this chapter is about the nature of glory. No one denies that worship is about humans glorifying God. The issue is whether God is primarily concerned about glorifying himself, or whether the God who is love is inherently a self-sacrificial Being rather than a self-aggrandizing One. What do you think?

2. Revelation 4 is a crucial passage for any theology of New Testament worship. It makes very clear that the worship of all

We Have Seen His Glory

creatures, both great and small, should be God-centered, not audience-focused. Worship is about giving God his due, what he desires and requires, not what the congregation wants and craves. List some of the pitfalls of a consumerist approach to worship.

3. In this chapter I maintain that worship completes the life cycle of all creatures. In Revelation 4, animals, humans, and angels are all lifting up God, bowing before God. How does this vision of worship change the way you think about it?

4. In Isaiah 6, when the prophet encounters God, he realizes his uncleanness, but that gets remedied in his worship encounter. How do you think one should prepare to come into the presence of a holy God? Is it OK to be casual about it? What do you think it means when God says, through the psalmist, "Be still and know that I am God"?

5. What does it mean to be "in the Spirit on the Lord's Day"? Why is this important for true worship?

CHAPTER THREE

Worship as Sabbatical

 The most valuable thing the Psalms do for me is to express the same delight in God which made David dance.

C. S. Lewis

On This Day, at This Hour

Too seldom noticed in discussions of worship is that worship, whether in the Old Testament or in the New Testament, is on the sabbatical plan — the one-in-seven schema. But why? In the last chapter we talked a good deal about the relationship of the creation order and worship, and how worship is a way that creation and, more specifically, human creatures recognize and affirm that creation order. But there is another way that this is so.

Let's recall the story of creation in Genesis 1 — how it was all in a week's work for God, and how on the seventh day God "rested" (or, more literally, "ceased") from his creating activity, and was profoundly pleased with the results, declaring it *tov m'ov* — very good. Worship is an eschatological act in the sense that in a fallen world, worship restores order and recognizes the original divine design of space and time. Worship, then, is not only reflecting back on the original creation, but also looking forward to the new creation, and in a sense is one of the interim acts that gives a foreshadowing and a foretaste of the restoration of all things. Just as we celebrate the Lord's death until he comes, so also we celebrate both the past mighty acts of God and also, in advance, the restoration of creation order, the sabbatical pattern. We celebrate into the final rest of God and creature in the Kingdom.

Exodus 19–20 has something to say on this matter. It tells us that God commissioned Moses to go and tell the people that he was coming down in a cloud of glory and that they needed to prepare themselves for the day; in this case the text says, "Be ready for the third day." The people were to sanctify themselves and their clothes, and husbands were to abstain from sexual activity with their wives. So God came down for this close encounter of the first kind, and the people were all warned to stay away from the holy mountain itself, lest they get "zapped." God then came and gave his people the Ten Commandments, the longest of which by far is the commandment about the Sabbath. Here is what it says in Exodus 20:8-11:

> Remember the Sabbath day by keeping it holy. Six days you shall labor and do all your work, but the seventh day is a Sabbath to the LORD your God. On it you shall not do any work, neither you, nor your son or daughter, nor your manservant or maidservant, nor your animals, nor the alien within your gates. For in six days the LORD made the heavens and the earth, the sea, and all that is in them, but he rested on the seventh day. Therefore the LORD blessed the Sabbath day and made it holy.

In a later chapter we will have occasion to say something about the relationship of worship and work, of ceasing and doing. But here our focus must be elsewhere. Suffice it to say that worship is a form of service to God (hence the phrase "worship service"), just as work is a form of service to God, so it is not a contrast between activity and inactivity, or labor and rest. Indeed, both worship and work are mandates, commandments of God, and so both are ethical acts when we respond appropriately, and they are not optional ethical acts, either.

Here we must focus on the fact that the connection between the original creation order and worship are made perfectly clear. We worship and rest on the day that God did. Simple enough. And it would thus necessarily be the seventh day, sundown on Friday to sundown on Saturday. But here is one of the very clear places where we see that the eschatological order of things and the Christian reality which is based on it are meant to be rather different. We live out of the new creation order which is already but not yet, the Kingdom which is already but not yet, and in worship we pray it will finish coming.

On a bright April morning, probably in A.D. 30 (or 33), there was a new tomb on the edge of Jerusalem which was quickly vacated. This happened not because the occupant was going on a heavenly vacation, ceasing entirely from his earthly labors, but because he had been quickened by the Spirit, because he had been summoned to begin the eschatological age. In short, he had been resurrected. And, unlike previous persons raised from the dead, Jesus was the first to experience the future eschatological condition, being given a resurrection body.

Once the one and only Messiah and Savior of the world was resurrected, life could not go on as if it were business as usual. The eschaton had broken into human history, into space and time, and there was no stopping the coming of the Kingdom now. Jesus' resurrection was not an isolated event in the midst of human history. It was, as Paul calls it, the firstfruit of the resurrection — the beginning of the End. And make no mistake, the End will not be just a recapitulation of the pre-Fall Beginning. One of the ensigns of this fact is that Jesus died just before the Sabbath began, but he rose on Sunday morning. Henceforth, new life would replace old life, new ways would replace old ways, new patterns would replace old patterns as the paradigm for the future and the proof that happy days were here again.

Of course, it was always true that the Sabbath was made for the good of humankind, that humankind was not made for the Sabbath, however good it was and is (Mark 2:27-28). But suppose that now that Christ has come — and indeed, the risen Christ has appeared — we find our rest not in the absence of activity but rather in the presence of the Lord?

In Matthew 11:28-30, Jesus, taking on the words and the guise of Wisdom, tells his disciples to take up his yoke (as opposed to that of the Torah), and he will give them rest. He personally will do it. The *shalom* he is referring to involves not a minus sign but rather a plus sign — value added. It means what *shalom* really means — peace in the sense of the healing, living presence of God which gives one rest from one's ills and makes one whole. This, of course, is why Jesus healed on the Sabbath repeatedly. What more perfect day to give people rest from what ailed them?

$(+)$

plus
sign

value
added

But when we get to Easter morning, something else has happened as well. Death, not merely disease, has been overcome. Christ came to reverse the curse as far as the curse was found — and of course the ultimate wages of sin was death. Easter is a death-defying day, and our Savior is a death-defying Lord. The earliest Christian confession seems to have been that Jesus is the risen Lord. And this changes everything — including worship.

While one can say, in broad strokes, that Old Testament worship was grounded and founded in the Passover/Exodus/Sinai events, New Testament worship is rooted in the Christ event, including especially his death and resurrection, but rooted also in his coming again, to complete the eschatological tasks and ring down the curtain on old kingdoms, bringing Kingdom Come in its fullness. We live between the first Easter and the last one, between new birth and new body, and our worship should reflect where we stand in the eschatological calendar of events.

This is why I would stress that it is no accident that the language about the day of worship carefully mirrors the language about what happened on that first Easter morning. This is especially clear if we compare even disparate texts by different authors such as Mark 16:2 and parallels, and Acts 20:7. The former says that quite early on the "first day of the week" (more literally, "the first of the Sabbath," or, better said, "the first day after the sabbath") the women went to the tomb and found it empty. Echoing this phrasing almost exactly, Luke says in Acts 20:7 "but on the first of the Sabbath, they came together breaking bread." This was indeed the habit of the earliest Christians. They had a new worship day, in addition to synagogue worship, and they kept it regularly. This is precisely why Paul says in effect at 1 Corinthians 16:2, "Now on the first of the Sabbath each of you should set aside/reserve what God has prospered you with for the collection." Alms were collected on worship day, when the community gathered, and this practice was considered just as crucial a part of worship in early Christian circles as it was in early Judaism. (See Acts 2 and 4 on the earliest Christian meetings.) Equally important is Revelation 1:10, where John of Patmos says, "I was in the Spirit on the Lord's day [*te kuriake hemera*], and I heard. . . ." Now we have a Christian name for the day, replacing the phrase "the first of the sabbath," and if we go only a little bit further beyond John's time into the early second century, around A.D. 112, we have an outsider's clear witness that Christians got up early on a fixed day of the week, and sang hymns to Christ "as to a god":

> They were in the habit of meeting on a certain fixed day before it was light, when they sang in alternate verses a hymn to Christ, as to a god, and bound themselves by a solemn oath, not to any wicked deeds, but never to commit any fraud, theft, or adultery, never to falsify their word, nor deny a trust when they should be called upon to deliver it up; after which it was their custom to separate, and then reassemble to partake of food — but food of an ordinary and innocent kind. (Pliny, *Letters*, 10.96)

What is most telling about this description is not merely the reference to a fixed day, but the time — "before it was light." The very same language is used of the women's visit to the tomb. The point is this: from the outset, Christian worship, unlike synagogue worship, was in the morning, not at sundown. It was not viewed as a mere recapitulation of Old Testament worship, and the timing of it makes this clear. Even more crucially, whereas worship *could* be held at any time of day (Jews had various hours of daily prayer which could be extended into fuller forms of worship), the reference to the morning provides a clear allusion to the Easter story. Christians would worship on the Lord's Day, what was called Sunday, and so begin a new practice, not merely repristinate or continue an old one. In short, the Easter event itself is what changes the day of worship and turns it into an event which should focus primarily on the new creation order, not the old one. And this brings up a collateral point. The women were the first witnesses to the risen Jesus, and Mary Magdalene was the first proclaimer of the Easter message. It could hardly be clearer that the ministers of Easter would be different from the priests who administered the old covenant worship.

Negative confirmation of the point I'm making comes from the various Pauline warnings not to go back to the Jewish calendrical celebrations. Colossians 2:16-17 in fact says that Christians should *not* get caught up in the Jewish festivals, the new moon celebrations, and the Sabbaths *because* they are but shadows of the coming things; the body of Christ is where one finds the substance. I take it that Paul is referring to the fact that the Christian meetings where the body gathered were where one could see the fulfillment of what God intended for worship, which the old worship practices only foreshadowed. In this view, Paul had company in the writer of Hebrews. One can also consult Galatians 4:10-11, where Paul makes a similar point to the one in Colossians 2:16-17.

The days of Sabbath worship, the days of priests, sacrifices, and Temple worship, while not perhaps over for all Christians, were nonetheless eclipsed by the reality of Easter worship. Christians were to live out of and into "Kingdom Come," out of and into the resurrection, and the ensign of this change was the new day on which they met. In *The Ways of Our God*, Charles Scobie concludes, "For the first three centuries the church observed Sunday as the day of worship, but *not* as a day of rest, and the identification of Sabbath and Sunday is relatively late."[1]

The New Meaning of Sacrifice, Priest, Temple

When it comes to worship patterns, change comes hard. Old traditions die hard, if they die at all, and sometimes Christians wind up being glorious anachronisms of an earlier age of worship. We often kid that the seven last words written over the lintel of the sanctuary ought to be "We've never done it that way before." It's a pity, because Christian worship is meant to be eschatological in character, and forward-looking. I'm reminded of the parody of an old Christian hymn:

> Backward Christian soldiers,
> Marching as to war.
> Sisters we are treading
> Where we trod before.

> Not united brothers,
> Not one Body we.
> We will all be standing here
> Until eternity.

1. Charles H. H. Scobie, *The Ways of Our God: An Approach to Biblical Theology* (Grand Rapids: Wm. B. Eerdmans, 2003), p. 610.

One of the most remarkable transformations or trans-valuation of values is the way that the language of sacrifice, temple, and priest is changed from the Old Testament to the New Testament. Let us begin with Romans 12, perhaps one of the earliest clear emblems of the change. In Romans 12:1 Paul uses the religious language of sacrificial ritual to talk about the posture of Christian living as an offering of self up to God and in service to others, especially one's fellow believers. The second word out of Paul's mouth is *appeal* rather than *command*. Paul is a good rhetorician, and he knows that it is far better to persuade than to command if it accomplishes the same end, especially when one is addressing an audience that one for the most part did not convert! There is a place for imperatives, but they need to be embedded in a discourse where appeal and persuasion are the main instruments used, especially in a situation such as Paul is in when writing to Roman Christians, most of whom are certainly not his converts and would not necessarily instantly recognize his authority over them.

Paul begins by appealing to the audience to offer themselves up to God. In fact, he argues that they must offer their very bodies to God, because of course their bodies are the vehicles through which they act and behave in various ways. The body, the whole self must become a living (as opposed to a dead) sacrifice, one which is holy and acceptable and pleasing to God. A sacrifice, of course, entailed the whole creature, the whole body, so the word *body* is apposite here.

Animal sacrifices are no longer necessary in view of the once-for-all sacrifice of Jesus, but it is precisely *that* "human" sacrifice of Christ which provides a pattern for Christian behavior, which is meant to be cruciform. One must offer one's whole self up to God, just as Jesus did on the cross, and indeed, God will accept no substitutes. The process of substitution came to a climax and completion in the death of Jesus.

Paul then suggests that this is the audience's reasonable or logical worship. Once one has presented oneself in this way to God, one's life, one's time, one's behavior, and one's beliefs are no longer one's own; all belongs to God. The sacrifice no longer has a final say over its own behavior. He or she is now God's property. Paul could hardly have put things more clearly: God doesn't merely want something *from* us — he wants us!

Worship, by definition, is where the creature recognizes that he or she is a creature and God alone is the Creator. Worship is an act of submission, of placing oneself under the deity. This, of course, also implies a denial of one's own divinity, a denial that one is lord over one's own life. If one has done this, then it follows that one has committed oneself to following the dictums which logically follow in this discourse. While some Christians may have felt, and do still feel, they could do nothing to please God, this text says otherwise. Paul says that Christian worship, obedience, holiness, and unity do indeed please God. While those in the "flesh" cannot please God (Rom. 8:8), those in the Spirit can indeed do so. Notice as well that worship is not merely any sort of obedience but rather total surrender, presenting one's whole self as a living sacrifice. Once the offering is on the altar, there is no going back — it is now God's property. Christians are not their own anymore; they have been bought with a price and have been asked to lay themselves on the altar.

Perhaps you've heard the old farmer's story about the difference between making an offering and offering a sacrifice. The hen and the pig are having a conversation in the barnyard, and the hen is moaning and groaning because the farmer wants two eggs for breakfast. "I guess I'll have to make a sacrifice," she laments. The pig, hearing this, snorts and says, "Sacrifice! You're only making an offering. The farmer wants bacon for breakfast too, so I'm the one who'll be making the sacrifice here!" Paul doesn't appeal to the audience to give an offering — that doesn't require the giving up of the whole self. No, Paul says that true worship involves presenting oneself as a living sacrifice to God.

Notice as well that Paul is talking here about a worship that is worthy of thinking beings. This is not unthinking or blind devotion, but rather worship based on what we do indeed know and recognize to be true about God. I suspect that Paul is speaking in a way that the Romans could have well understood. Epictetus, the Stoic philosopher so much admired by many Romans, once said, "If I were a nightingale, I should be singing as a nightingale; if a swan, as a swan. But as it is, I am a rational being; therefore I must be singing hymns of praise to God" (*Discourses*, 1.16.20-21). Philo said something similar: "The soul . . . ought to honor God not irrationally nor ignorantly, but with knowledge and reason" (*Special Laws*, 1.209). N. T. Wright may be correct as well in pointing out that Paul is saying that this behavior is only logical in light of the arguments about the character and saving activity of God given in Romans 1–11.[2] This brings up a key point. The coherency and consistency of Paul's ethic presupposes and depends upon the coherency and consistency of his theology. If one does not accept the latter, one is unlikely to be persuaded by the former. In short, if one's theology of worship isn't sound, one's ethical practice of worship is hardly likely to be sound, either.

Romans 12:2 offers a stark contrast with verse 1. One is not to be conformed but rather transformed. This evil age tries to mold a person into a particular shape. Paul believes that while Christians must live in this world, in this eschatological age, the form, pattern, and dominant Zeitgeist of this world is nonetheless passing away. It is thus foolish to be conformed to something which is on the way out and already has the odor of death. Paul then urges that believers live in this age while not allowing its mind-set and habits of the heart to dominate their thinking and behavior. The verbs *conform* and *transform* here are in the present continual tense in Greek, thus referring to a constant and ongoing process

2. N. T. Wright, "Romans and the Theology of Paul," in *Pauline Theology*, vol. 3, ed. D. M. Hay et al. (Minneapolis: Fortress Press, 1995), pp. 30-67.

that requires one to work at de-enculturating oneself and re-orienting oneself. There is perhaps a real point to using the two verbs chosen. To be conformed is to allow oneself to be socialized by outside influence. But being transformed is an inward process, in this case administered by the Holy Spirit.

Since it is the mind which is being transformed, Paul is clearly talking in the first instance about a change of worldview, but he is also referring to a change in the affections and the will as well. The Christian must look at the world through the eyes of Christ. And the beginning of the process of mental renewal comes when one has a true conception of the true God. It is this mental renewal which leads to presenting one's body for sacrifice. Recognition leads to religion. But Paul also stresses that the renewal of the mind is the necessary prerequisite to discerning God's will and thus believing and behaving in a way that glorifies God and edifies others.

It cannot be stressed enough that in his ethicizing Paul honors the minds and hearts of his audience. He doesn't just expect them to be obedient; he expects them to develop a capacity for Christian moral discernment. For many — perhaps most — situations in a Christian's life, there is no biblical rule on page 93 that one can turn to and know exactly what to do. Therefore, one needs to have a renewed mind and a clear moral vision, and to develop a competency in making good moral choices, choices that are good and pleasing to God. And of course worship, good worship, is always pleasing to God.

Discerning what is good, pleasing, and perfect in God's sight is often difficult in a fallen world. This process of ethical discernment is what Sam Wells calls "improvisation."[3] However, Romans 12:3 makes evident that the Christian is not alone in his or her moral reflections. Paul's ethic is an ethic of and for the Christian

3. Sam Wells, *Improvisation: The Drama of Christian Ethics* (Grand Rapids: Brazos Press, 2004).

We Have Seen His Glory

community, and there is a need for them to come and reason together about such things. But of course, for such team thinking to happen, there must be actions and attitudes which promote an environment where Christians can live together in peace and harmony and think and work together.

One of the problems that Paul had to deal with in this particular case was hubris (see Rom. 11:25). Pride and arrogance on the part of some Gentile Christians were causing problems in their being reconciled with the minority Jewish Christians. Paul thus calls his audience to sober-mindedness, to thinking neither more highly nor more lowly than they ought about themselves. The terms used here refer to soundness of mind, sober, honest reflection, discretion, and moderation. Verses 3 and 6 are where Paul says that God has bestowed different kinds and degrees of abilities on different persons, and indeed, even different measures of faith. Though many commentators have sought to escape the conclusion that Paul actually says this, a careful comparison of verse 3 and verse 6 makes this clear, as does looking at other examples where Paul uses the verb *merizo* (1 Cor. 7:17; 2 Cor. 10:13). We should not really be surprised by this, since Jesus himself could speak of those who had little faith and those who had great faith.

Paul is saying that believers need to evaluate themselves on the basis of what gifts they have been given and their "measure of faith." A person could be greatly gifted but have little faith; the converse is also possible. Another possibility is that one could have both great faith and great gifts — a great combination. Here "faith" does not refer to saving faith, the faith that led one to believe in God in the first place. Rather, it has to do with the level of one's trust as a Christian in God, or perhaps some special sort of faith such as the degree of faith needed to be an agent of healing (see 1 Cor. 12–13). This discussion of the measure of faith serves as the guide for the following discussion of gifts and how they should and shouldn't be exercised.

Notice, however, the order of things in this discussion. Paul talks about a theology of worship and sacrifice first, and then addresses the issue of gifts and graces. Too seldom is this the order of things in modern-day conversations about worship and its participants. We take the *America's Got Talent* approach to deciding who does what in worship. Paul says that the prerequisite is having given oneself totally to God, and then recognizing the character and measure of one's faith. The transformation of the mind happens in this process of worship, because worship above all other acts causes us to re-evaluate ourselves and give ourselves a reality check.

We could spend a considerable period of time examining Hebrews 6–10 and learning about how Christ's death put an end to all literal sacrifices and made them obsolete, including the good ones offered in early Judaism. In Hebrews, Christ's sacrifice is said to be once and for all, making all other such literal sacrifices otiose and pointless. Indeed, if one was to undertake them, it would be a repudiation of what Christ accomplished on the cross. Paul, of course, is prepared to go so far in taking the language of sacrifice and applying it to Jesus and his death that at 1 Corinthians 5:7-8 he says boldly, "for Christ is our Passover sacrifice." Christians don't need to celebrate Passover past any longer; they need to celebrate Christ our Passover, who fulfills all these previous festivals and celebrations in his death and resurrection.

Though not quite like Paul, the author of Hebrews still draws the same conclusions as Paul when he says in Hebrews 13:15 that Christians should simply offer the sacrifice of the praise of their lips. We may compare as well 1 Peter 2:5, where Peter uses the very term "spiritual sacrifices" — in fact, he goes the whole nine yards of spiritualization, saying, "As living stones you are being built into a spiritual house unto a holy priesthood offering spiritual sacrifices, well-pleasing to God through Jesus Christ." Notice that Peter is referring to all believers here, and later in 1 Peter 2, as priests, all offering spiritual sacrifices, and all being built into a spiritual form of God's house.

It is interesting to closely examine Hebrews 12 as well, where the author contrasts the theophany at Sinai, to which we can't and shouldn't return, and the future Christophany, when Christ returns to raise the dead and judge the world. The author says that we must draw nigh to the latter Christophany and not go back to the former one. He is exhorting us to face forward into the future and worship, anticipating the return of Christ. He puts it this way at Hebrews 12:22-24:

> But you have come to Mt. Zion, to the city of the living God, the heavenly Jerusalem. You have come to thousands upon thousands of angels in joyful assembly, to the church of the firstborn, whose names are written in heaven. You have come to God the judge of all, to the spirits of the righteous made perfect, to Jesus the mediator of a new covenant, and to the sprinkled blood that speaks a better word than the blood of Abel.

In many ways, this passage is similar to the vision of heavenly worship that John recounts in Revelation 4–5.

What the author of Hebrews is telling us is that what is currently "up there" will one day be "out there" at the eschaton, for heaven and its inhabitants are coming down, and there will be a corporate merger of heaven and earth as the new Jerusalem descends to earth. Then heavenly worship will become earthly worship indeed. Christian worship here and now has a vision of what is up there, and knows that one day it will be on earth, and so it faces forward into the future, knowing that Christ in us provides the hope of glory and the assurance that the consummation herein described is coming, and that we should be worshipping our way into it as the church expectant, which will one day become the church triumphant.

Since Christ's death is a once-for-all sacrifice for all sins for all times, literal sacrifices are not needed anymore, and literal priests are out of work. And since the function of sacrifices was to reconcile the worshipper with God, and Christ has now permanently accomplished this reconciliation, there is no longer a need for a temple or temple apparatus. No need for literal altars, no need for lavers to wash animals, no need for the slaughtering of the lambs, because the once-for-all slain Lamb stands sentinel in heaven and presides over a new eschatological order of things (Rev. 5).

Paul is just as clear as Peter about the people of God being the temple and body and dwelling place of God. 1 Corinthians 3:16-17 is a crucial text, making clear that "you [plural] are God's temple in which God's Spirit dwells." Or we could consider 2 Corinthians 6:16: "We are the temple of the living God." Strikingly, this is said of the individual in 1 Corinthians 6:19-20. The metaphor of the Temple as building is applied to the church in Ephesians 2:20-22, just as it is in 1 Peter 2:4-10. God is no longer localized in a building. God is present wherever his community is found, wherever two or more are gathered.

This did not mean that Christians would not continue to meet in buildings — first in homes, then in homes modified for worship, and eventually in structures built especially for worship when Christianity was no longer a proscribed "superstition" in the Roman Empire. We will have occasion to say more about this a bit later in this study. This new temple and new priest theology also did not mean that Christians would be leaderless in worship; Paul and his co-workers and the local house-church leaders served such functions. But they were not singled out as literal priests.[4]

Even when Christians shared the Lord's Supper together, they did not see it as a literal sacrifice or as a recapitulation of Golgotha, or a re-presenting of Christ to God. Did they believe that some sort of real spiritual transaction happened when Chris-

---

4. Notice the spiritualizing of the priestly role in Romans 15:15-16, where Paul says he has the priestly duty to proclaim the Gospel to Gentiles so that he can offer them up to God as a sacrifice.

tians partook of the elements in a worthy fashion? Yes, they did.[5] But they did not conceptualize it in terms that erased the differences between Old Testament and New Testament worship. That would happen considerably later in Christian history, and at great cost. An Old Testament hermeneutic of literal priest, temple, and sacrifice took over, reversing the spiritualizing process we see in the New Testament, and leaving behind, among other things, women as ministers, on the logic that since women couldn't be priests, they couldn't offer the Eucharist, and if they couldn't offer the Eucharist, they couldn't be ministers.

But when ministers become priests, and the Lord's Supper once more becomes a sacrifice, and churches become temples, and Sunday becomes the Sabbath, what it means is a rejecting of the New Testament theologizing and hermeneutic in regard to these things, a rejecting of eschatological worship when it comes to these things, and a going back to the old trodden paths of the Ancient Near East of patriarchal priests, temples, and sacrifices. If we follow their example, we have rejected new creation-order worship for the old creation-order worship. Instead of looking forward toward the eschaton, we have chosen to turn around and look backward, and back our way into the future. And this, frankly, is a backwards way to do things, to give up being an Easter people heading for the New Jerusalem, where there will certainly be no temple, no priests, and no more sacrifices. In our next chapter we must ask a probing question: What did early Christian worship, living in the shade of Easter and the shadow of the eschaton, actually look like? What did worship between the already and the not yet of the Kingdom involve?

5. See Witherington, *Making a Meal of It: Rethinking the Theology of the Lord's Supper* (Waco, Tex.: Baylor University Press, 2007).

Questions for Reflection and Discussion

1. Why do you think that worship is on a sabbatical plan, according to the Bible — a one-in-seven schema?

2. Do you see the Lord's Day as the same thing as the Sabbath? Why or why not? What is the difference between a day of rest and a day of worship?

3. In what sense was the Sabbath made for human benefit?

4. According to the New Testament, what sort of sacrifices, priests, and temples are appropriate for Christians and their worship? In what sense does worship restore creation and creatures to their proper place?

5. What does Paul call our logical or reasonable worship in Romans 12?

CHAPTER FOUR

The Legacy of Judaism

As worship begins in holy expectancy, it ends in holy obedience. Holy obedience saves worship from becoming an opiate, an escape from the pressing needs of modern life.

Richard Foster, *Celebration of Discipline*

The first element in worship is adoration. The Hebrews expressed this by their posture and not alone by their word, for they prostrated themselves before God. "O come, let us worship and bow down: let us kneel before the Lord our Maker." They did not come with an easy familiarity into the presence of God, but were aware of His greatness and majesty, and came with a sense of privilege to His house.

H. H. Rowley, *Worship in Ancient Israel*

Jesus and the Jewish Heritage

All of the earliest Christians were, in fact, Jews. As Jews, and especially if they were Jews who lived in or around Jerusalem, they did not cease to go to the Temple for prayers, to the festivals, to the synagogue. Why should they? They didn't see their newfound faith in Jesus as somehow the start of a new world religion; indeed, they saw it as the natural messianic development of Judaism. Furthermore, though Jesus had clearly criticized the Herodian Temple in Jerusalem and had foreseen its demise, he had not suggested to his followers that they stop worshipping in synagogues, or even stop going to the Temple.

When Luke gives us a glimpse of the life of Jesus between his birth and his adult ministry, some interesting things come to light. As a young man, Jesus called the Temple his Father's house in Luke 2:49 — or did he? The Greek here is elliptical. It reads literally, "Why were you seeking me? Didn't you know that it was necessary for me to be in the . . . of my Father?" Did it mean that Jesus had to be about his Father's business, as some translations would have it, or that he had to be in the house of his Father? It appears to me that the latter is likely meant, not least because Jesus is perfectly comfortable with being there, and later in his ministry, with teaching there. Furthermore, in the Sermon on the Mount, a text like Matthew 5:23-24 suggests that Jesus accepts the Temple as part of the current order of things. Jesus, at least during his earthly life, did not initiate a new pattern of worship.

Perhaps more pertinently, Jesus seems to have preached, taught, and healed in synagogues in Galilee with some regularity during his ministry (see, e.g., Mark 6; Luke 4), and since even in Acts we find Christians going to the synagogue (including Paul's going there first for evangelism), it is useful to ask two questions: What was the legacy of Jewish worship to earliest Christian worship? And what was the overall legacy of the synagogue to the early church in terms of leadership, structure, patterns, and the like?

The synagogue was not a place of priests and sacrifices, and it was no temple. It was not an institution run by priests or Levites. Only in Jerusalem was there a high priest and a temple cultus. Worship anywhere else in Jewish territory looked different.[1] The synagogue was a meeting place for worship and for instruction and dialogue (the *bet'ha midrash*), which was begun probably in exile, or in the period shortly thereafter, for Jews who had no place to meet and no Temple to visit. One must realize that whatever happened in Babylonian exile, worship still went on. We know this for a fact because there are various psalms written from and for worship in exile (see, e.g., Psalm 137). It will be wise to have a brief discussion about the rise of synagogues and the character of the worship there.

The Rise of the Synagogue and the Rise of Christianity: Was there an Edifice Complex?

One of the major debates in New Testament studies in the past fifty or so years has been when and where synagogues — which is to say, purpose-built religious structures — began to crop up in Israel or the Diaspora. At one point there were numerous New Testament scholars who were emphatic that there were no such purpose-built structures during or before the New Testament era. This in turn led to the insistence that what we see in the Gospels and Acts, which refer to synagogue buildings with some regularity, reflects the later conditions of the authors, in some cases from late in the first century outside Israel, and then within Israel. In other words, the New Testament writers were accused of anachronism at best. Here is a good example of how New Testament scholarship is sometimes done either by blithely ignoring the archeological evidence or by castigating it as ambiguous or irrelevant, while attempting to explain it away.

1. The Samaritans, of course, had Mt. Gerizim and sacrifices there. In fact, they still do, to this very day. But this is of no relevance to our discussion, since Jews were not involved there, and would not attend worship there. Not even Jesus, with his various forays into Samaria, is ever said to be involved in worship at Gerizim.

Dr. Lee Levine came forward — in writing, in Society of Biblical Literature sessions, and elsewhere — and made it emphatically clear that there were indeed purpose-built synagogues even in Jesus' day and thereafter, and that in fact the practice may well predate the Herodian era. One of the sites that Levine used as a cornerstone of his argument was in the lower Golan Heights, at the village of Gamla, sometimes also called Gamala (from the Hebrew word for camel, because the hill on which the village rests looks like the hump or perhaps the nose of a camel from a certain angle). As it turns out, Levine was absolutely right.[2]

The village of Gamla seems to have begun as a Selucid outpost in the second century B.C. A fort was established there as a sort of early warning signal for those living in the Holy Land. It apparently became a civilian settlement of Jews sometime later in that century. Our main interest is in the village's religious life and the excavation of the synagogue at Gamla, which is very substantial indeed. This building can rightly be compared to what has been found at Masada, Sepphoris, Capernaum, and elsewhere in the region. Why is this important for New Testament studies?

In the first place, the archeological evidence removes the necessity for the argument that Acts reflects second-century Jewish religious life, not first-century conditions. My own observation is that when people have questioned the historical accuracy of New Testament remarks about buildings and historical locales, time and again the New Testament has eventually been vindicated by the archeological evidence. This should give pause to scholars who too hastily want to argue alternate cases, merely dismissing the evidence of the New Testament about such things.

The importance of the Jewish evidence becomes apparent when we also want to raise the question of what the earliest Christians would have thought about purpose-built structures. All of

2. See Lee Levine, *The Ancient Synagogue: The First Thousand Years* (New Haven: Yale University Press, 2005).

We Have Seen His Glory

the earliest followers of Jesus were Jews, many of them were devout, and certainly most of them would have attended worship services in synagogues in Galilee and elsewhere, as the clear evidence suggests that Jesus did as well.

Jesus was highly critical of the Herodian Temple not because it was a structure built with human hands but because God's house had been turned into a den of thieves. In other words, Jesus renewed the prophetic critique not about constructing buildings but about corrupt practices within them when they were supposed to be houses of prayer and sacrifice.

Similarly, in the important book *Hebrews and Hellenists,* Craig Hill quite convincingly shows that Stephen in Acts 7 is not "Temple critical" or "Torah critical"; he is critical of God's people, who kept killing the prophets and failing to live by God's Word. In other words, Jesus and his earliest followers did believe that the Herodian Temple might well be the Temple of Doom, destined to be destroyed by God — again, not because it was a building but because of the corruption within the building and its human administration. Jesus and Stephen were not early examples of anti-edifice preachers, nor were they iconoclasts. Rather, they were devout early Jews who didn't want the House of the Lord, whether synagogue or Temple, polluted by wicked practices.[3]

If we turn then to the evidence of Acts 1–6 and ask about the views of the earliest Christians about religious buildings, it seems clear that they didn't have a problem with them in the least. Peter and other Christians continued to hold meetings in Solomon's Portico in the Temple. Paul continued to attend worship in synagogues — indeed, he began his evangelistic efforts in a synagogue wherever he went — and when he returned to Jerusalem, he gladly participated in support of Nazaritic vows and rituals in the Temple at James's request, despite the danger to his own life (see Acts 21). Of course, it is also true that Jewish Christians met in

---

3. Craig Hill, *Hebrews and Hellenists* (Minneapolis: Fortress Press, 1991).

homes, as did Gentile Christians later. Legally speaking, there became an increasingly good reason to do so, as the first century marched along and it became more and more clear that Christians were not simply Jews, or a sect of Judaism.

Judaism in the first century was a licit religion. Jews were allowed to have their own temple and sacrifices, and they were not required to sacrifice to the emperor; rather, the distinction was made that they could offer prayers and sacrifices on behalf of the emperor. Even though anti-Semitism was rife throughout the Empire, the official Roman policy was to allow indigenous groups to continue to practice their religions, as long as they were ancient, respected, identifiable religions, recognized by the Roman senate. Judaism was such a religion.

However, as the first century wore on and more and more Gentiles became followers of Jesus, even becoming the majority of such followers in various places in the Empire, it became increasingly clear that the *Christianoi,* the partisans of Christ or those who belonged to Christ (a name first given to them by outsiders in Antioch) were not simply Jews. This in turn made them practitioners of what Romans called a *superstitio,* an illicit religion. Now this was a difficult thing for Christians, not least because, unlike Judaism, early Christianity was a highly evangelistic religion, even recruiting from the highest echelons of society, something to which Luke in Acts draws repeated attention. But if pagan officials thrust them out of the synagogue and would not allow them to meet in the open because of being a "superstition," where would they meet?

Of course they would continue to meet in homes. This was not made a religious principle; rather, they had to make a virtue out of a necessity. The movement had to continue to grow and expand without constantly being subject to the watchful eye of governing officials, who increasingly wanted to promote an alternative new religion: the cult of the emperor. Thus, when the parting of the ways came with the synagogue, Christians met increasingly

We Have Seen His Glory

in homes. The fact that this was not a theological issue or principle but rather a practical one is shown so very clearly already when Christians began to turn homes into churches in the last third of the first century in places like Capernaum, and when they began already in the second century to build underground church structures in places like Turkey.

The underground churches in Turkey were built between the late first century and the fourth century, which is to say, between the time when Nero began persecuting Christians and when that practice stopped when Constantine became emperor and declared Christianity a licit or legal religion. Clearly, Christians engaged in this practice to protect Christianity and allow it to grow and thrive. The church literally met underground in structures that were often enormous and elaborate.

What is interesting to me about the actual structures of these underground churches is that they have adopted some of the features of the synagogue — for example, niches in the back of the structure for their holy scrolls — and some features from the home, such as the little tricliniums (couches) with benches that allowed for the sharing of a meal, including the Lord's Supper.

What I need to stress is that Christians didn't build underground homes; they built underground church structures in these places. They continued to live above ground, but they would meet either in well-walled houses or underground spaces during these difficult centuries. They had no problems with constructing purpose-built structures with synagogue features, and increasingly they used their own architectural and Christian designs. They did not hold to theological principles which suggested that edifices built for worship were inherently bad and worship in houses was theologically better.

The notion that there was some enormous sea change in attitude about buildings between the time of earliest Jewish Christianity and the time when Gentiles made up the majority of Christians is a myth, a myth of pristine origins followed by later pagan corruption.[4] In fact, there was a continuum from earliest Christianity onward in which Christians were happy to meet in synagogues, temples, or homes, wherever they were welcome and could worship in spirit and truth. But once Christians had been branded as practitioners of a false superstition by Nero and later emperors, they were increasingly removed from worship in synagogues, and this drove them to adopt and adapt, turning houses into purpose-built religious meeting places, and later building underground churches in areas where that was possible, such as Turkey.

The earliest Christians had neither an "edifice complex," insisting on religious buildings, nor an anti-edifice complex. They were flexible and practical, doing what was possible in a given place, always bearing in mind that once they emerged from the Jewish womb and were no longer seen as a part of Judaism, they were practicers of an illicit religion and had to be careful where, how, and when they met. Open, above-ground meetings in urban areas became increasingly impossible because they would be noticed. Bear in mind the famous letter of Pliny to Trajan that we have already referred to, written in about A.D. 111-12 from Bithynia. Christianity was a faith under fire, and Pliny asked for advice about what to do with Christians and whether they should be forced to renounce their faith. I want to give the full text of the letter here, as it reveals the dilemmas that Christians faced specifically in regard to worship — not merely in continuing to worship Jesus but in avoiding worship of the emperor.

XCVII

Pliny to Trajan:

It is my constant method to apply myself to you for the resolution of all my doubts; for who can better govern my dila-

---

4. This myth was sadly perpetuated by Frank Viola and George Barna in their recent polemical book, *Pagan Christianity* (Carol Stream, Ill.: Barna-Books, 2007).

We Have Seen His Glory

tory way of proceeding or instruct my ignorance? I have never been present at the examination of the Christians [by others], on which account I am unacquainted with what used to be inquired into, and what, and how far they used to be punished; nor are my doubts small, whether there be not a distinction to be made between the ages [of the accused], and whether tender youth ought to have the same punishment with strong men? Whether there be not room for pardon upon repentance? Or whether it may not be an advantage to one that had been a Christian, that he has forsaken Christianity? Whether the bare name, without any crimes besides, or the crimes adhering to that name, is to be punished?

In the meantime, I have taken this course about those who have been brought before me as Christians. I asked them whether they were Christians or not? If they confessed that they were Christians, I asked them again, and a third time, intermixing threatenings with the questions. If they persevered in their confession, I ordered them to be executed; for I did not doubt but, let their confession be of any sort whatsoever, this positiveness and inflexible obstinacy deserved to be punished. There have been some of this mad sect whom I took notice of in particular as Roman citizens, that they might be sent to that city. After some time, as is usual in such examinations, the crime spread itself, and many more cases came before me.

A libel was sent to me, though without an author, containing many names [of persons accused]. These denied that they were Christians now, or ever had been. They called upon the gods, and supplicated to your image, which I caused to be brought to me for that purpose, with frankincense and wine; they also cursed Christ; none of which things, it is said, can any of those that are ready Christians be compelled to do; so I thought fit to let them go. Others of them that were named in the libel said they were Christians, but presently denied it again; that indeed they had been Christians, but had ceased to be so, some three years, some many more; and one there was that said he had not been so these twenty years. All these worshipped your image, and the images of our gods; these also cursed Christ.

However, they assured me that the main of their fault, or of their mistake, was this: — That they were wont, on a stated day, to meet together before it was light, and to sing a hymn to Christ, as to a god, alternately; and to oblige themselves by a sacrament [or oath] not to do anything that was ill: but that they would commit no theft, or pilfering, or adultery; that they would not break their promises, or deny what was deposited with them, when it was required back again; after which it was their custom to depart, and to meet again at a common but innocent meal, which they had left off upon that edict which I published at your command, and wherein I had forbidden any such conventicles. These examinations made me think it necessary to inquire by torments what the truth was; which I did of two servant maids, who were called Deaconesses: but still I discovered no more than that they were addicted to a bad and to an extravagant superstition. Hereupon I have put off any further examinations, and have recourse to you, for the affair seems to be well worth consultation, especially on account of the number of those that are in danger; for there are many of every age, of every rank, and of both sexes, who are now and hereafter likely to be called to account, and to be in danger; for this superstition is spread like a contagion, not only into cities and towns, but into country villages also, which yet there is reason to hope may be stopped and corrected. To be sure, the temples, which were almost forsaken, begin already to be frequented; and the holy solemnities, which were long intermitted, begin to be revived. The sacrifices begin to sell well everywhere, of which very few purchasers had of late appeared; whereby it is easy to suppose how great a multitude of men may be amended, if place for repentance be admitted.

Trajan replied to this now-famous letter as follows:

XCVIII

Trajan to Pliny:

You have adopted the right course, my dearest Secundus, in investigating the charges against the Christians who were brought before you. It is not possible to lay down any general rule for all such cases. Do not go out of your way to look for them. If indeed they should be brought before you, and the crime is proved, they must be punished; with the restriction, however, that where the party denies he is a Christian, and shall make it evident that he is not, by invoking our gods, let him (notwithstanding any former suspicion) be pardoned upon his repentance. Anonymous informations ought not to be received in any sort of prosecution. It is introducing a very dangerous precedent, and is quite foreign to the spirit of our age. (Pliny, *Letters*, 10.96)

In his important Cambridge monograph *From Synagogue to Church*, James T. Burtchaell demonstrates beyond a reasonable doubt the indebtedness of early Christians to the synagogue in three ways: (1) in terms of their worship practices; (2) in terms of their leadership structures, particularly in regard to the roles of elders; and (3) in terms of their thinking about and adaptation of what religious buildings should look like, and how they should be constructed.[5] His essential point should be stressed: It was not paganism or even the influx of Gentiles into the early church that led to its having purpose-built structures, hierarchical leadership structures, or structured worship practices. These things existed from the beginning in earliest Christianity because of its deep indebtedness to early Judaism, and its theology, praxis, and attitudes

5. James T. Burtchaell, *From Synagogue to Church* (Cambridge: Cambridge University Press, 1992).

about worshipping God and how to do it properly. These things also existed because there was indeed a hierarchy of leadership (all Jews at the outset) in the early church from the apostles on down, involving apostles and apostolic co-workers at the top, then prophets and teachers and evangelists of various sorts (all of the aforementioned tended to be itinerant), then local church overseers, elders, deacons, prophets, pastor-teachers, and others.

It is, of course, also true that early Jewish Christians added important things to the earlier Jewish mix when it came to leadership and religious structures, worship patterns, and the like. Early on, Jewish Christians began to have their own religious symbols, such as the IXTHUS symbol. But innovation is only what one would expect from a pneumatic or charismatic movement like early Christianity. Since the Gospel was to the Jew first, and also to the Gentile, as even the apostle to the Gentiles insisted (see Rom. 1:1-4 regarding his practice in Acts), Jews brought into the church their own religious ethos and practices, including, of course, their beliefs and praxis in regard to worship, leadership, and buildings.

It is always a delicate thing to understand and represent the balance between the continuity and discontinuity in these matters that Judaism and Christianity shared. The point is that early Christian worship, leadership, and attitudes about religious structures were not simply what the Romans would call a *novum*, something totally new. This is precisely why outsiders, when they attended Christian worship in homes and elsewhere, often remarked on the Jewishness of what they experienced.[6] It was unlike paganism and polytheism in many ways. And yet, and yet, it was not quite what they had come to associate with Judaism because of the significant focus on Jesus of Nazareth, even to the point of praying to and worshipping him.

---

6. R. L. Wilken, *The Christians as the Romans Saw Them* (New Haven: Yale University Press, 2003).

We Have Seen His Glory

The Synagogue and Early Christian Worship: The Overlap

We have mentioned above James Burtchaell's conclusion that earliest Christianity was indebted to the worship practices of early Judaism. But what were those practices prior to the disastrous Jewish War in the sixties and the demise of the Temple in A.D. 70? We must assess this matter cautiously because we know that after A.D. 70 there began to be a reassessment of things in early Judaism, at least in regard to the necessity of priests, temples, and literal sacrifices. Nevertheless, a few things are clear.

In the synagogue service there was singing, there was praying, there was reading of Scripture, there was exposition of Scripture (and there might also have been response or dialogue with the congregation thereafter), and there was almsgiving. And apparently the service was concluded with a benediction of some sort.

While the synagogue was normally a place for Jews and God-fearers and proselytes to worship, Jesus apparently saw the Temple itself as having from the outset a broader intended audience in this regard: *it was a house of prayer for all peoples.* Notice his quoting of Isaiah 56:7 in his critique of the mercantile activities in the Temple during the last week of his life (Mark 11:16-17). What is noteworthy to me is that every one of these sorts of activities can be chronicled as transpiring in the early Christian meetings, as well as some other more pneumatic activities.

If we examine, for example, the summary passages in Acts 2:44-47, we find reference to prayers; sharing of food (including making sure no one was in need, which entailed selling possessions and goods); praising God (v. 47); and continuing in the apostles' teachings. The additional element, of course, is the meeting in each other's homes and breaking bread there, and the commitment to share all things in common together (*koinonia*).[7]

7. This term should not be translated as "fellowship," though practicing it could result in fellowship. What it means is sharing or participating in something together.

Equally, we could turn to Acts 4:32-35, which gives us a summary of these early meetings. What is made clearer in this summary, at verse 33, is that the apostles' powerful witness "about Jesus and the resurrection" was a part of these meetings, as well as what went on in the Temple courts. What is also clear is that, as in the synagogue, there was a leadership structure. The laying of goods or funds at the apostles' feet so that they could distribute these alms (vv. 34-35) makes this quite apparent. Of course, the disciples continued to meet in Solomon's Portico in the Temple precincts to bear witness and to evangelize, but it would be a mistake to think that preaching and teaching did not go on in the house meetings as well. We see this clearly later in Acts in the famous Eutychus story (see Acts 20:7), where it says that "on the first of the Sabbath when they were gathering together in one place to break bread, Paul preached to them for a prolonged time [beyond midnight]."

Some of the content of the preaching "in house" would have been different from the content in a synagogue or in the Temple precincts, but what is noteworthy about what we find in Acts is that it is the *leaders* doing the preaching and evangelizing, whether in the houses, in the synagogues, or in the Temple. (Compare Acts 20:7 with Acts 2–4, and notice the repeated pattern of Paul and Apollos and others preaching in the synagogue — e.g., Acts 18.) This brings us to the point where we ought to say something about synagogue elders and their functions, as opposed to, say, a Jairus-like figure who might be a ruler or president and so presider in a synagogue.

While it is certainly true that the term *presbyteros* might simply refer to an old person in a Jewish context — or, for that matter, in a Christian context (see 1 Tim. 5:1-2) — it normally had a religious content in Christian contexts (see Titus 1:5).[8] This is not

---

8. Notice how, when the author wants to simply refer to older men in 1 John 2:12-14, he uses the term *fathers* to distinguish them from younger men and youth.

We Have Seen His Glory

surprising, since this term came into Jewish Christianity first from the synagogue (see, e.g., Acts 15:1-6 — the elders of the Jerusalem church). It is interesting that when Paul actually wants to characterize himself as an elderly person, he uses a different form of this word: *presbytes* (Philem. v. 9).

So when, for example, Paul called the elders of Ephesus (i.e., the leaders of that church) to come meet him at Miletus, he wasn't asking the senior citizens of that church to go on a long walk to meet him! More often than not, the term *elder* in the New Testament refers to a church role, function, office — call it what you like. And this shouldn't surprise us, since there already were such folks in the synagogue who were not necessarily graybeards.[9]

What is true, however, is that elders, while they might not have been elderly, nonetheless were adults with some life experience, and to judge from the Pastoral Epistles, this trend continued on the missionary field as well, which explains why Paul insisted on married men and women filling the offices of elder and deacons. The culture had a strong bias in favor of age and experience, and the church had to deal with this. This is precisely why Paul had to encourage Timothy and exhort him, "Don't let them despise your relative youth" (1 Tim. 4:12).

Listen to a literal reading of Acts 14:23: "Paul and Barnabas appointed [or ordained] elders for them in each church . . . and committed them to the Lord." It seems clear, at least in early Christianity, that it was the apostles and the apostolic co-workers who appointed the elders, the overseers (who seem also to have been elders, though not all elders were overseers), and the deacons. This is the way that both Acts and the Pastoral Epistles depict things. What this in turn means is that leadership did not simply arise indigenously within the original house churches, though we certainly do see other factors besides apostolic appointment coming into play. For example, there were more pneu-

9. See the discussion in James Burtchaell's *From Synagogue to Church.*

matic roles — the role of prophet, for instance — and there were roles that were taken up for social and practical reasons: Philemon had a house in which a church could meet, and he became a house church leader in his own home. In other words, the leadership structure of early Christianity was partly traditional and deriving from synagogue practice, partly practical, and partly pneumatic.

It is a mistake to take a text like 1 Corinthians 11–14, where Paul was correcting all sorts of problems in the Corinthian church, and see that as a model of how things were or ought normally to have been done in an in-home Christian worship service. Paul was trying to bring some order out of the chaos there and was busy asserting his own authority over that congregation and situation, even to the extent of demanding the expulsion of a member, silencing some in worship, telling the congregation what the protocol must be for the communal meal, and the like.

IN THIS CHAPTER we have emphasized the continuity factor between early Judaism and early Christianity, but we must take a closer look at the discontinuity factor as well. What is not always recognized is that we have considerable evidence within books other than Acts about what went on in early Christian worship. First, some of the so-called letters in the New Testament are actually sermons to be delivered in house churches (e.g., 1 John, James, and Hebrews). Second, even those documents which have epistolary frameworks were intended to be rhetorical discourses delivered orally to congregations during worship, which explains why so many of these documents begin with a prayer (a thanksgiving prayer) and end with a benediction or doxology, neither of which features were typical of ancient letters. These Christian "letters" were meant to serve as the sermon or teaching or discourse for house church meetings, and as we already saw in the case of Acts 20:7, in-house sermons could be very long indeed. Third, the epistolary corpus and other New Testament documents contain fragments of prayers, Scripture citation and exposition, creedal statements, and hymns that reflect the worship life of early Christianity. It is to these latter elements of Christian worship that we want to turn first in our next chapter. Christian worship was hovering between the already and the not yet, between what had come before in the synagogue and the new thing that had been spawned by the Christ event and the coming of the Spirit. Christian worship was not a complete "novum" which would have been unrecognizable if a God-fearer or Jew or knowledgeable Gentile came in and observed what was happening. But clearly the new and distinctive element was what made it stand out most from worship in the synagogue.

Questions for Reflection and Discussion

1. What practices did the earliest Christians carry over from the synagogue? What can Christians learn from this?
2. In this chapter, one of the things I emphasize is that there was no great sea change in attitude toward worship spaces and buildings between the time of earliest Jewish Christianity and the time when Gentiles made up the majority of Christians. Why is it important to understand this?
3. One of the carryovers from Judaism to early Christianity was a hierarchical leadership structure. How did and does this affect worship? Early Judaism also influenced purpose-built worship structures and structured worship practices. Why is it important to recognize this influence?
4. What role should elders have in leading worship? Do you think the role of elder is gender-specific?

CHAPTER FIVE

Glorifying God in a Bolder Way

Since I am coming to that holy room,
Where, with thy choir of saints for evermore,
I shall be made thy music; as I come
I tune the instrument here at the door,
And what I must do then, think here before.

John Donne, "Hymn to God, My God, in My Sickness"

Spirit-filled Singing

Christians today are used to addressing God in shockingly familiar and even casual ways. Some even talk to and about God as if
God were a long-lost pal. What always strikes me about the stark
contrast between what happens so often today, especially in
prayer, and what we find in the New Testament is that the New
Testament writers were looking for the most exalted language they
could possibly find to pray and praise and proclaim God's goodness and grace in a bolder way. There was not prose or even poetry
elevated enough to do justice to the subject of Christ and the redemption he wrought. Looking for help, the earliest Christians
turned to the Psalter and other such musical resources.

Ephesians 5:18-20 provides a glimpse into the heart of early Christian worship, which, surprisingly enough, the New Testament writers do not say enough about. Paul, in a circular homily meant for a variety of his churches, says this in instructing them about worship: "Don't become intoxicated with wine, in which is recklessness, but rather continue being filled with the Spirit, singing to one another psalms, hymns, and spiritual songs and making melody in your heart to the Lord, giving thanks always for everything in the name of our Lord Jesus Christ to [our] God and Father." It will be wise for us to look closely at this passage.

In verse 18 we have a clear contrast: Don't get drunk with wine (Paul doesn't say "Don't drink wine" but rather says "Don't engage in dissipation"), but instead be filled with the Spirit. This contrast is also found in the Pentecost story in Acts 2 and suggests that early Christian worship was often ecstatic and jubilant, involving loud singing. The outsider might have had a hard time telling the difference between exuberant praising (especially if it involved singing in tongues) and drunken singing and carousing. It is not impossible that Paul is contrasting Christian worship with Bacchic rites, which involved drunkenness and frenzy and orgiastic behavior.[1] In any case, it should be noted that Paul says to Christians who already have the Spirit, "be filled," and the verb is in the present continual tense in Greek: keep on being filled up by and with the Spirit. The phrase "wholehearted singing" or even "exuberant singing" doesn't do justice to what is being described here. Christians are wide open to the internal workings of the Spirit, and the result is, both internally and externally, a kind of deeply vibrant expression almost beyond words.

Here Paul is likely referring to the sort of repeated fillings that happen to Christians who already have the full measure of the Spirit but are inspired in spiritually "high" moments to speak and

1. See C. L. Rogers, "The Dionysian Background of Eph. 5:18," *Bibliotheca Sacra* 136, no. 1 (1979): 249-57.

sing. In such cases it is a matter of the indwelling Spirit inspiring and lifting up these believers, not a matter of their getting more of the Spirit. They are caught up in wonder and love and and praise and adoration of God by the Spirit, who moves them.

John Chrysostom is right in suggesting that Paul is contrasting intoxication, which leads to one sort of singing, and inspiration, which leads to another. Paul is not talking about some second work of grace or of sanctification here, as the contrast makes clear. "For they who sing psalms are filled with the Holy Spirit, as they who sing satanic songs are filled with an unclean spirit. What is meant by 'with your hearts to the Lord'? It means with close attention and understanding. For those who do not attend closely merely sing, uttering the words, while their heart is roaming elsewhere" (*Homilies on Ephesians,* XIX). Paul means singing from the bottom of one's heart, and so this is an exhortation to sincere, heartfelt praise and singing, with cognizance of the lyrics' meaning.

There's a difference between mere ecstatic uttering of nonsensical things and heartfelt praise, which is an act of adoration. Perhaps Paul knew about the Dionysian rituals in which getting drunk was seen as the means of achieving religious ecstasy or frenzy or spiritual exaltation (cf. Isaiah 28:7; Philo, *De Ebrietate,* 147-48; *Vita Contemplativa,* 85, 89; Macrobius, *Saturnalia,* I.18.1; Hippolytus, *Refutation of All Heresies,* 5.8.6-7). Since early Christian worship took place not only in the context of homes but also often in the context of fellowship meals, the issues of drunkenness and worship were not unrelated for Pauline Christians, as 1 Corinthians 11 also demonstrates.

As Gordon Fee points out, what often gets overlooked in the discussion of Ephesians 5:18-21 is that we have a series of participles that modify the exhortation to be filled by/with the Spirit — speaking, singing, giving thanks, submitting.[2] The Spirit inspires

---

2. Gordon D. Fee, *God's Empowering Presence* (Peabody, Mass.: Hendrickson, 1994), p. 719.

all these activities. Fee also rightly notes that the emphasis here is not on the ecstasy-producing potential of the Spirit but on being filled, or having the fullness of the Spirit's presence.[3] Nor is the emphasis on being "high" or drunk on the Spirit as opposed to being drunk from wine. Rather, the picture is of individuals and a community together being totally given over to the Spirit and the Spirit's presence and leading.

Philo seems to describe something of the life situation Paul has in mind here:

> Now when grace fills the soul, that soul thereby rejoices and smiles and dances, for it is possessed and inspired, so that to many of the unenlightened it may seem to be drunken, crazy, and beside itself. . . . For with those possessed by God not only is the soul wont to be stirred and goaded as it were into ecstasy but the body is also flushed and fiery . . . and thus many of the foolish are deceived and suppose that the sober are drunk. (*De Ebrietate*, 146-48)

Being filled with the Spirit, therefore, doesn't lead to dissipation or drunkenness. On the contrary, Paul affirms that it leads to wisdom and to a sound mind and to the proper adoration that all of God's creatures should render to God. In other words, it is the key to living the Christian life in a manner pleasing to God and edifying to others as well as oneself.

The Spirit is both the means and the substance of the filling, and verse 19 tells what sort of response the Spirit prompts in the believer. Christians sing hymns to Christ and also give thanks to God through the impulse and empowering of the Spirit. Note the implicitly Trinitarian nature of this discussion.[4] The life of the

3. Fee, *God's Empowering Presence.* See also A. J. Kostenberger, "What Does It Mean to Be Filled with the Spirit? A Biblical Investigation," *JETS* 40 (1997): 229-40.

4. Fee, *God's Empowering Presence,* pp. 721-23.

Spirit-filled community is to be characterized by joyful singing, thanksgiving, and submitting to one another. Harold Hoehner comments, "If believers were only filled with wisdom, the influence would be impersonal; however, the filling by the Spirit adds God's personal presence, influence, and enablement to walk wisely, all of which are beneficial to believers and pleasing to God. With the indwelling each Christian has all of the Spirit, but the command to be filled by the Spirit enables the Spirit to have all of the believer."[5]

It is possible that the three sorts of songs mentioned in verse 19 had differing forms. *Psalmos* probably means "the psalms," usually praise songs with accompaniment, since the term originally meant "to pluck a string." *Hymnois* may mean hymn-like liturgical and a cappella pieces which were pre-written. Spiritual songs may mean spontaneous songs from the heart prompted by the Spirit. We can't be certain about any of this (cf. Col. 3:16).

What these verses suggest is both old and new elements in Christian worship when it came to music. Paul says, surprisingly enough, that Christians are to address these songs to each other as well as to God! They are to speak to one another in songs of praise. This makes clear that worship is not just a matter of adoration, but also involves edification. Verse 19c probably doesn't mean praising "only in your hearts" but rather "in a heartfelt way," the understanding being that the praise is ultimately offered to the Lord. Perhaps the text means that the internal praise is offered to the Lord, but the external praise is offered to each other. We are always to do this in the spirit of thanksgiving (cf. 1 Thess. 5:18), and we are to do it submitting ourselves to one another. It is not to be a protracted display of ego, and, as 1 Corinthians 14 suggests, believers are to defer to each other, taking turns.

Notice too that here, as in 1 Corinthians 14, nothing suggests

5. Harold Hoehner, *Ephesians: An Exegetical Commentary* (Grand Rapids: Baker, 2002), p. 705.

We Have Seen His Glory

a clergy-dominated worship service. Everyone is allowed to join in and participate as the Spirit leads them. However, we would be wrong to think that this was leaderless worship, for Paul has just listed for us in Ephesians 4 the various leaders of these sorts of congregations when an apostle was not available: prophets, evangelists, and pastors who are also teachers (Eph. 4:11). Their job is the equipping of the saints unto the building up of the body of Christ, and certainly worship is one of the activities which accomplishes that building up and unifying of a group of Christians. Can we say more about the music itself? I believe we can.

The parallel passage in Colossians 3:16-17 bears close scrutiny. Verse 16 indicates that the basis of sound and wise teaching and admonition is the word of Christ dwelling in the midst of the community richly. Notice that this exhortation is given to everyone, and the assumption is that this is as appropriate when predicated of all as when these terms are used in Colossians 1:28 to describe Paul's ministry. This exhortation is not directed, for instance, just to the men of the audience, any more than the next exhortation about singing is. Once again, three types of songs seem to be referred to: psalms, hymns, and spiritual songs. Psalms would presumably refer primarily to the Old Testament songs we find in the Psalter; hymns could be said to refer to the kind of Christological material we find in Colossians 1 (it certainly refers to something sung to a deity); and spiritual songs would refer to songs prompted by the Holy Spirit, perhaps spontaneously. The grammar allows the conclusion that singing is viewed as one form of teaching and admonishing each other,[6] and certainly Ephesians 5:19 mentions speaking the songs to one another. Colossians 1 reveals Paul using a hymn for just such an instructional purpose. According to verse 17, the Christian life is also to be characterized by being and showing oneself thankful for all God has done, and

6. See Fee, *God's Empowering Presence*, pp. 649-56.

by doing and saying everything in the name of and according to the nature of Christ.

When we see singing under the heading of instruction and exhortation, it becomes clear once more that worship is seen as an ethical act, and one aspect of this is that as God is glorified properly, the people are edified. What Paul emphasizes here is that these songs express the Word of God, which is to dwell richly in the speaker and singer. Singing is quite specifically connected here with admonitions. But the end of verse 16 makes clear that the ultimate aim of this expression is "singing in your heart to God" — or, perhaps better said, singing wholeheartedly unto God. Verse 17 punctuates this even further when Paul insists that whatever we say or do, especially in worship, we should do in the name and according to the nature of Christ, giving thanks to the Father through Christ. Christ is seen as the mediator of our relationship with the Father, but here and in Ephesians 5 the implication is also that Christ is the object of worship and adoration.[7] This will become obvious as we examine now some of the Christological hymn fragments we actually have in the New Testament, which makes ever so clear that Christian worship was very much Christologically focused.

Christological Choruses

There was a very long history of singing in the Jewish tradition. In fact, we have evidence that it goes all the way back to the patriarchal period. We can point, for example, to the songs of Moses and Miriam (Exod. 15) and to the famous ode of Deborah (Judg. 5). These songs were primarily songs of adoration and celebration for what God had done for his people in the past, and so they had a

---

7. See Max Turner, "Ephesians," in *Theological Interpretation of the New Testament*, ed. Kevin Vanhoozer (Grand Rapids: Baker, 2005), p. 128.

flavor of salvation history. But it would be remiss to think that singing was one thing and praying another in the Hebrew tradition, because a great deal of the Psalter is sung prayers, even very ancient ones like the sung prayer of Moses in Psalm 90. The Temple cultus was built during the time of Solomon and thereafter, and there developed a considerable scribal process of collecting, sifting through, and creating material for the Temple singers to sing on various occasions. At the beginning of some of the psalms we even find instructions to the choir director in regard to tunes to be used when this or that song or sung prayer was to be performed (see, e.g., Ps. 80, Ps. 84). And clearly there were psalms written for certain occasions — for example, for the Sabbath (Psalm 92), for making the pilgrimage up to Jerusalem (the so-called psalms of ascent; see Pss. 120-134), for the coronation of a king (Ps. 2), and for entrance into the city (the psalm provided a kind of liturgy of entrance; see Ps. 24:7-11). There were different kinds of psalms: songs of praise, songs of thanksgiving, songs of creation (Ps. 8), songs about the law (Ps. 119), songs of penitence (Ps. 51), and songs of intercessory prayer (Ps. 59). It is perhaps surprising to discover that psalms of lament or complaint made up the single largest category of songs.

These songs were metrical and had tunes assigned to them. They were for both choral and congregational singing, and they were part of a larger liturgy connected with the various Jewish festivals and special days. One can imagine Psalm 51 and many other penitential psalms being sung on the Day of Atonement. When we turn to the New Testament, however, something interesting happens. While the vast majority of Old Testament songs are purpose-driven and topical in nature, some of them provide a bit of a review of salvation history or celebrate a theophany of God, and some of them are quite specifically said to be for teaching (Ps. 78). Israel sung its theology and ethics, and so we will not be surprised to learn that early Christians did so as well.

Thus it is important to say clearly that those references to singing psalms in Colossians 3 and Ephesians 5 are more important than they may have first appeared when it comes to assessing early Jewish Christian worship. These references make it very apparent that there was a carryover of Old Testament worship modes into the Christian celebration. They too sang the psalms of old, and by doing so sang songs that endorsed the traditions of having choirs and choir directors and liturgies and instruments (Ps. 150:3-4). And of course the whole association of the Psalter with David, a musician who played some kind of lyre for Saul and others, reminds us that Christians took over a musical tradition that was by no means a purely a cappella one.

Our focus here needs to be on the new hymns that Christians wrote, and it must be noted from the outset that all of them are paeans of praise to Christ. Christ was the heart and most distinctive element of early Christian preaching, and, predictably, Christ was also the heart of early Christian singing, and so of worship. It will serve us well to examine the character of these hymns, of which we have only fragments in the New Testament.

Let me say at the outset that we should not be surprised by this development. Already in the Aramaic-speaking Jewish Christian community in Jerusalem, Christians had been praying to Jesus as God. We see this in 1 Corinthians 16:22b — *marana tha*, they pled — which, translated from the Aramaic, means "Come, O Lord." Now, you don't pray to a deceased rabbi to come back, but you do pray to the risen Lord to return. Praying to and praising Jesus as God was apparently part of the very earliest Christian worship life. This explains why many scholars have long surmised that the high Christology we find in the New Testament arose out of worship life, and indeed out of the personal experiences of the earliest Christians in worship. Theology as doxology and doxology as theology has a very long pedigree in the Christian tradition.

Bearing these things in mind, let's take a look at these hymns. We'll start with what is in some ways the most complete of these hymn fragments: Philippians 2:6-11:

We Have Seen His Glory

Who, being in the form of God,
Did not consider the having of equality with God
Something to be taken advantage of,
But rather stripped/emptied himself,
Taking the form of a servant,
Being born in the likeness of human beings.
And being found in appearance like a human being,
He humbled himself, being obedient to the point of death —

Even death on the cross.

That is why God highly exalted him
And gave him the name, the one above all names,
In order that at the name of Jesus
All knees will bend —
those in heaven, on earth, and under the earth,
And all tongues confess publicly that Jesus Christ is Lord
Unto the glory of God the Father.

What we notice about this hymn fragment is that it presents the story of Christ in the form of a V pattern: pre-existence in heaven, earthly existence, and exalted existence in heaven again. The pre-existent Son gives up his heavenly prerogatives and becomes a humble human being, even dying the most shameful of all human deaths on a cross. Paradoxically enough, it is precisely for all this self-humbling and even humiliation that God has exalted Jesus. (It would appear that hymns like this rarely mention the return of Christ.)

Other Christological hymn fragments of note are found in Colossians 1:15-20, 1 Timothy 3:16, and Hebrews 1:2b-4. And of course there is that great prologue hymn in John 1 about the *logos*, who is quite explicitly called God. Reading through this hymnic material, one gets the impression that the writers were looking for terms grand enough to express their feelings and their attitude of worship and adoration when it came to Christ. There had been a Copernican revolution in the thinking of these early Jews due to the Easter events, and this led rather rapidly to a Christological reformulation of monotheism which one can see as well in the remarkable Christian "Shema" in 1 Corinthians 8:6: "For us there is one God, the Father, from whom all things came and for whom we live; and one Lord, Jesus Christ, through whom all things came and through whom we live." This so clearly echoes Deuteronomy 6:4 — "Hear, O Israel: the Lord our God, the Lord is One" — only now the term *God* is applied to the Father and *Lord* to Jesus Christ. This shows just how profound a change had occurred in the thinking of devout Jews like Paul. Not even the odes of salvation history in the Old Testament give any hint of God sharing his praise or divine work with anyone else. The theophanies celebrated in the Old Testament have become eclipsed by the Christophany celebrated in these hymns in the New Testament.

We would love to know so much more about these hymns. When were they sung, to what sort of tunes were they sung, how often were they sung? But we must content ourselves with the knowledge that Paul, or the author of Hebrews, or the author of the Fourth Gospel could simply quote the familiar refrains of these hymns and expect the audience to chime right in, knowing what they were all about.

Here as well it is appropriate to consider the Christological doxologies and benedictions in the New Testament. The earliest is perhaps the one most like 1 Corinthians 8:6 in offering "doxa" to both the Father and the Son, found at the end of Jude in verses 24-25:

> To him who is able to keep you from stumbling and to present you before his glorious presence without fault and with great joy — to the only God our Savior be glory, majesty, power, and authority through Jesus Christ our Lord, before all ages, now and evermore! Amen.

Notice that the doxology or praise is offered through Jesus, and the concluding phrase would seem to suggest that the Lord had always been, is now, and always shall be. This is quite similar to the pronouncement in Hebrews 13:8: "Jesus Christ is the same yesterday, today, and forever."

Notice the exhortation just shortly thereafter in Hebrews 13:15: "Through Jesus, therefore, let us continue to offer to God a sacrifice of praise — the fruit of lips that openly profess his name." Jesus is not only the *mediator* from God to us through whom we have received salvation; he is also the *means* through whom we praise God, as both the verses in Jude and the verse in Hebrews indicate.

It is not surprising, then, that in a combined benediction and doxology in Hebrews 13:20-21 we find similar notions:

> Now may the God of peace, who through the blood of the eternal covenant brought back from the dead our Lord Jesus, that great shepherd of the sheep, equip you with everything good for doing his will, and may he work in us what is pleasing to him, through Jesus Christ, to whom be glory for ever and ever. Amen.

Notice again the "through" phrase at the end. Christ is due endless praise/glorifying, as the final words of the doxology say, but he is distinguishable from the God of peace as well. We may call these benedictions/doxologies examples of Binitarianism if we like — the worship of Father and Son — but whatever we call it, it reflects the change in worship patterns from those in the synagogue to those in the house churches. We could look at other such benedictions/doxologies (see, e.g., 1 Thess. 5:23-24 and 1 Peter 5:10-11), but we would be remiss not to note that it is here in these benedictions/doxologies that Trinitarian language may have first slipped into the discourse of Christian worship.[8]

8. It is worth noting again that these closing benedictions or doxologies

At the end of 2 Corinthians 13, for example, we have this benediction: "May the grace of the Lord Jesus Christ, the love of God, and the sharing in common of the Holy Spirit be with you all." We see, of course, a similar proto-Trinitarian thrust in the baptismal advice in Matthew 28:19. This Matthean verse is emphatic in that it says that the one name (not "names" plural) of God into which persons are to be baptized is Father, Son, and Holy Spirit. Liturgy and singing, initiation rites and benedictions — all coalesce to indicate the new Christian element being built on the foundation of the Jewish heritage adopted and adapted by the earliest Christians.

The new creedal fragments and confessions point in the same fresh Christological direction: the earliest explicitly Christian confession that one uses to proclaim that one is truly converted is "Jesus is the risen Lord" (Rom. 10:9). The earliest creedal statements stress that Jesus is both son of David and son of God (Rom. 1:3-4), both Jewish messiah and God blessed forever (Rom. 9:5). The eschatological age has come, but the past is not left entirely behind. Rather, the Jewish heritage is taken up into the new forms of worship and devotion and made to serve new ends and aims. But what about prayer life itself, more specifically? Was it simply pneumatic and spontaneous in character, or did it also at times have a form and a given shape?

Praying to *Abba*

In a revealing moment in Romans 8:15-16, 26-27, Paul gives us a glimpse of the inner workings of the prayer life of the earliest Christians. The Holy Spirit, says Paul, not only liberated Chris-

---

make clear the settings in which these so-called letters would be orally delivered: in worship. Ancient letters didn't have such religious benedictions, often closing with just a simple "Farewell."

tians from the bondage of sin and fear (see vv. 1-2), but also brought about the believers' adoption as children of God — indeed, heirs of God and co-heirs with Christ (v. 17). It is thus not a shock that this entitles Christians to pray to God as *Abba*, just as Jesus did. Paul puts it this way: "By [the Spirit] we cry *Abba*, Father. The Spirit himself testifies with our spirit that we are God's children." Of course, what is so fascinating about this is that Paul assumes that his Roman, largely Gentile audience will know exactly what he is talking about here — he and they both pray to God as "*Abba*, Father," even if they know not one other smidgen of Aramaic.

It is hard indeed to avoid the conclusion that they had been taught what we call the Lord's Prayer. Especially interesting, however, is Paul's assertion that the Holy Spirit prompts such an addressing of God as *Abba*. Then Paul admits that we need this help, that we are weak and do not know how to pray aright, but that the Spirit intercedes for us as well as prompts our own words (v. 26). Romans 8:26-27 could be a reference to glossolalia, something which Paul certainly believed in — the angelic prayer language (1 Cor. 13:1) which he himself used (see 1 Cor. 14, especially v. 18). Paul calls this sort of Spirit-impelled praying "praising God in the Spirit," but he urges praying with the mind as well. We must consider now the prayer that generated such prayer language.

Matthew 6:5-15 is probably the most familiar of all the passages in that Gospel; even today, its words are repeated weekly by Christians around the world. Prayer, fasting, and almsgiving were three of the pillar virtues or religious practices of early Judaism, and so it is not a surprise that these things are discussed together here in this sermon as well; what we should stress here is that we could call this part of the sermon Jesus' commentary on worship.[9] Just as Jesus suggests that fasting is not appropriate when the

9. There were, of course, other such pillar virtues: M. Avot has Torah, service, and deeds of loving-kindness.

bridegroom is present, but rather feasting, and almsgiving should look like the total sacrifice of the widow with her mite, not merely like tithing, so also he alters the Jewish religious prayer practice with a different sort of prayer.

It is wise to point out from the start that this is a prayer for the disciples, as taught by Jesus, so it really should be called the Disciples' Prayer, though one can make a case that Jesus prayed a form of this prayer in the garden of Gethsemane. Luke 11:1-2 says that one of the disciples actually asked Jesus to teach them how to pray, and perhaps we should see this as a request for a prayer that would characterize the disciple's life, and so not a prayer for all.

It is characteristic of the sort of wisdom discourse Jesus offered to give typical rather than exhaustive advice, and this prayer is no different. These are the *sorts of things* that followers of Jesus ought to pray about. Having told the disciples how not to pray (i.e., not like the hypocrites who draw attention to themselves with lengthy, showy prayers), Jesus then turns around and tells them how to pray. Like most every other piece of Jesus' wisdom, this one has an eschatological flavor to it. One prays with one eye on the horizon, watching for the Dominion to come on earth. But at the same time, Jesus offers this prayer with full conviction that the Dominion is already breaking into human history through his own ministry. Jesus also makes it clear that praying is to be a personal matter, not just a reciting of a rote prayer.

The prayer of a truly pious person should never be a performance; it should always be personal, whether it is a preformed prayer or a spontaneous one. Clearly a private venue is seen as most appropriate for a personal prayer. One sure way to avoid showing off while praying is to go into a private room and pray alone. Then the one praying has only an audience of One. Verse 6c says that when one prays in secret, the Father who sees in secret will "restore it to you," which suggests that the prayer may be that of a disenfranchised person, someone who has been wronged or defrauded in some way.

The prayer begins with an address of God as *Abba*. The prayer then presupposes a definite personal relationship with God, so much so that one can address God as Jesus does. Notice in verse 7 the contrast with the babbling of pagans when they pray — a mindless repetition of something over and over again.[10] Verbosity is contrasted with the conciseness of the Lord's Prayer. The prayer of polytheists in Jesus' day was frequently long-winded because they often recited numerous names of deities, being uncertain about who had blessed and who had blighted them; they also tried to butter up the deities by using grandiose words and concepts in their address, hoping to be heard because of their expansiveness.

By contrast, Jesus' disciples knew that there is only one deity worthy of prayer and worth praying to, and since this deity doesn't need to be informed of anything, one can be concise and straightforward. The point of praying is to share personally with God what is on one's heart and what one is committed to as well. Prayer thus establishes contact and allows the believer to seek God's will in the context of an intimate conversation. It seems clear that Matthew 6:9-13 and Luke 11:2-4 are two forms of the same paradigmatic prayer for disciples, with the Matthean form made "user-friendly" for public worship (hence the plural "our" and "us"). Precisely because this prayer is found both in a Gospel meant for Jewish Christians (Matthew) and in a Gospel meant largely for Gentile ones (Luke), and because these Gospels were written at different times and in different places, we may be confident that this prayer was believed to be an important paradigm for any and all of Jesus' earliest followers.

Further, according to the First Evangelist, this is a prayer for the community to share together. To begin, it is probably right to suggest that the Matthean form of this prayer is on the whole

---

10. A good example would be from the Mithras liturgy. See M. Meyer, "The Mithras Liturgy," in *The Historical Jesus in Context*, ed. A. J. Levine (Princeton: Princeton University Press, 2006), pp. 179-92.

closer to the original wording of the prayer. So, for example, "debts" in Matthew is likely closer to the original words in Aramaic than Luke's "trespasses." Sins are a form of debt, and in fact one could say that they leave us in God's debt when he forgives us. Luke's wording includes the concept of things owed but broadens it to include other things done wrong. The Matthean form of the prayer has the opening invocation to God followed by three "you" petitions (vv. 9b-10b), which in turn are followed by three "we" petitions (vv. 11-13a). The doxology was probably added later, when the prayer became a regular part of Christian worship. Indeed, I would suggest that the doxology underscores the understanding that this prayer was supposed to be a regular feature of Christian worship.

One of the first questions to be asked about this prayer is, Who is hallowing God's name? Is this a prayer that God will hallow his own name by bringing in the Dominion and establishing his will on earth? This is possible, but the eschatological character of the prayer makes this a less likely option. It is more likely that Jesus is thinking of the time when the Kingdom will come on earth and every knee will bow and every tongue will confess the glory of God the Father, such that God is indeed hallowed on earth as he already is in heaven. Thus I think that the eschatological and ethical character of this prayer makes it unlikely that God is both the subject and the object of this prayer. In fact, it is quite possible that Jesus is modifying the Kaddish prayer, which reads in part, "Hallowed be his great name in the world, and may his kingdom come in your lifetime and in your days." In this prayer the hallowing is clearly done by humans, but the reigning is done by God; such is likely the case in Jesus' prayer as well.[11]

Notice as well that heaven is seen as the dwelling place of

11. A. J. Levine has pointed out to me that a better translation of the beginning of the Kaddish Prayer would be "To be made great and to be made holy . . ."

God, and it is contrasted with earth. Jesus affirms quite clearly the Creator/creation distinction. God is seen not as merely part of the world, or simply present within and contained by the creation, but as standing over it and ruling it from above. Jesus is no pantheist. Jesus is also under no illusion that God's Dominion and will are already fully manifested on earth. Much of what happens on earth is not God's will at all. God's will, by definition, is perfectly done in heaven, but we still must be praying for that to be the case on earth. Praying in the shadow of the Kingdom must reckon with both the already and the not-yet dimensions of the Kingdom's coming.

Verse 11 is the most controversial line of this prayer because of the word *epiousion* (which means either "for tomorrow" or "daily"). The debate boils down to two possible translations: either "the bread for tomorrow" or "daily bread." In either case, the prayer is for the necessary sustenance to live, symbolized here by bread, which was the most important staple of ancient diets. If one goes with the former translation, we are dealing with a family that needs the bread today, or else they will have no breakfast tomorrow. For this reason, some have seen this prayer as the last prayer of the Jewish day (prayer normally being offered anywhere between three and five times a day). In any case, this petition indicates the need to depend on God daily, even for the basic necessities of life.

The petition for forgiveness involves "debts," but since the word *forgive* is used, we may assume that more than financial shortcomings are in view. This petition stresses the connection between our forgiving others and our being forgiven by God. A person who refuses to forgive should not expect to receive forgiveness when the Dominion comes. The parable of the unmerciful servant extends the lesson into a full analogy in Matthew 18:21-35. If an individual will not offer forgiveness to others, he impedes receiving forgiveness in his own life. Once again Jesus is emphasizing the point that after someone becomes a disciple, his behavior will indeed affect his final status in the Dominion of God. The comments in verses 14-15 are not about initial forgiveness at conversion but rather about final and eschatological forgiveness. This is why verse 15b reads, "your Father *will* not forgive your sins."

Verse 13 is another controversial petition. Is there a contradiction here of what James says in James 1 about God never tempting anyone? After all, this prayer is directed to God. One may think of the example of Jesus, who was led into the wilderness by the Spirit but was tempted by Satan. Here is where we note that the word *peirasmos* in Greek can mean either "tempt" or "test," and of course the classic distinction is that God tests a person (e.g., Job), while the Devil tempts a person. Yet in the case of Job, it was the very same calamities that were both a test and a temptation. God meant it as a test, for a test is intended to strengthen one's character, but Satan meant it as a temptation in his attempt to destroy the man's character.[12]

Perhaps, then, the best translation here is "Do not put me to the test, but deliver me from the Evil One." There's an old Jewish wisdom prayer that reads, "Do not bring me into the power of a sin, a temptation, a shame" (*B.T. Ber.*, 60b). Similarly, this petition in the Lord's Prayer is probably asking God to protect the believer from temptation and Satan. It is interesting that the abstract concept of evil is nowhere mentioned in the New Testament — only "evil deeds" or "the Evil One." Evil always has a personal face in the New Testament. Turning evil into a mere power or force is a modern preoccupation. Many — probably most — early Jews clearly believed in a personal devil and in demons as well (cf. Matt. 5:37 and 13:19). The very things petitioned for in this prayer are things Jesus brought to those around him: daily sustenance, forgiveness, liberation from Satan, the doing of God's will on earth. This provides evidence that it is already God's will to provide these things.

One of the most important things about the Lord's Prayer is

---

12. Compare, for example, the remark of Joseph: "What you meant for evil, God intended for good" (Gen. 50:20).

We Have Seen His Glory

that it suggests what our priorities ought to be in praying. First and foremost is praising or hallowing God's name. Then we ask for God's will to be done and his divine saving activity to come on earth. Then we finally do pray for ourselves. We pray for the truly critical things in life: daily bread, forgiveness, the ability to forgive others, deliverance from temptation and the Evil One. In other words, we pray for both the physical and the spiritual necessities of life. Seeing the Lord's Prayer as a model prayer should lead us to ask if the priorities of our other prayers match up well with the priorities of the model. Indeed, we might well ask if what we are praying is something Jesus would pray, as he certainly would the Lord's Prayer. Perhaps we would do well to see invoking Jesus' name at the end of a prayer as signing his name to our petitions. If so, then we need to ask, Would Jesus sign off on our entreaties?

For our purposes, several features of this prayer help us to see something of Jesus' vision of worship and also what he expected his disciples to carry forward into the future. First, he expected them to live with great expectations in regard to the coming of God's eschatological Kingdom on earth, and that brought a certain eschatological sanction and seriousness to the need to be in deadly earnest about following Jesus' teachings to the letter. When one is praying for the Kingdom to come and God's will to be done once and for all on earth, one is praying not for just any sort of divine intervention, but rather for the final divine intervention. Here we may think of the famous parable of the persistent widow in Luke 18:1-8. Jesus is urging his disciples to persist in prayer, even if things don't appear to be going well, and he suggests at the end of the parable that the real question is not whether the Kingdom and its King are coming, but whether he will find true faith on earth when he arrives. Worship which involves the Lord's Prayer provides a constant reminder that the eschatological clock is ticking, and so the need to follow the instruction manual is paramount.

Second, the prayer begins in intimacy and ends in the ecstasy of adoration. It begins with the indication of intimate relationship with God, addressing God as *Abba,* and it ends with doxological thanks that God has the presence and the power to bring in his reign once and for all on earth. The worship inspired by Jesus takes this for granted and assumes that we should be as in earnest as God is about the coming of the Kingdom on earth. Worship which assumes that life will just go on day after day, as it always has, is *not* true worship, which keeps one eye on the horizon, looking for the return of the Savior.

Third, living between the already and the not yet of the eschatological situation means that we need to have our priorities straight: worship and the praise of God come first! Praying for God's will and reign to come on earth is the next priority. Praying for our own basic needs for daily bread and forgiveness comes next, and is intertwined with our willingness to share these staples, which feed the body and the human spirit.

Fourth, there is a realism to this prayer. The disciples will face serious temptations and tests along the way. In those tests they will need deliverance from the ultimate source of those temptations, the ultimate eschatological problem: the Evil One. Jesus the exorcist believed that it was part and parcel of his ministry to deliver people out of the clutches of the powers of darkness. This was a crucial part of the significance of the incoming of the divine, saving reign of God. Christian worship should be about celebrating that victory through the finished work of Christ, and this prayer already points the disciples in that direction.

Finally, the doxology, whether original to the prayer or not, is something that properly ends worship, for it once more recognizes that God is God, that in his hands are the presence and power and the future always, and believers must live on the basis of that realization. Worship is about a reality check — it is about recognizing that God is God, and only God can truly save the world, and this is precisely why only God is worthy of worship, for only the Creator is also the Redeemer. Accept no substitutes. And yet the assumption of this prayer is that disciples can participate in the final victory of God on earth by praying, for God has chosen to use the prayers of his people to help bring about that final deliverance, that final reign on earth.

If there were space and time, it would be worthwhile at this juncture to look at another early Christian document, called the *Didache,* deeply indebted to Matthew, and probably written for Jewish Christians toward the end of the first century A.D. In some ways it provides us with a clearer glimpse of how early Christian life and worship were undertaken by at least some early Christians. For example, it gives us the first clear instructions on how to perform Christian baptism, as well as some help with the Lord's Prayer. But our interest here is in the rich prayer material found in Chapter 10 of the *Didache,* which reads as follows:

Prayer after Communion

(1) After the meal, give thanks in this manner:

(2) We offer thanks, Holy Father,
For Your Holy Name which fills our hearts,
And for the knowledge, faith, and eternal life
You made known to us through Your Servant;
Yours is the glory forever.

(3) Almighty Master, You created all things for Your
    own purpose;
You gave men food and drink to enjoy,
That they might give You thanks;
But to us You freely give spiritual food and drink,
And eternal life through Your Servant.

(4) Foremost, we thank You because You are mighty;
Yours is the glory forever.

(5) Remember Your Body of Servants,
To deliver it from everything evil,
And perfect it according to Your love,
And gather it from the four winds,

Sanctified for Your kingdom, which You have prepared for it;
For the power and glory are Yours forever.
(6) Let Your grace come,
And let this world pass away.
Hosanna to the God of David!
May all who are holy, come;
Let those who are not, repent.
Maranatha. Amen.
(7)But permit the prophets to make Thanksgiving/Eucharist
as they wish.

What is immediately evident in reading this prayer is its indebtedness to the Lord's Prayer, and now we notice as well when such a prayer would be said — namely, after the Lord's Supper, which seems appropriate. Notice as well the inclusion of the Aramaic prayer *marana tha,* which we have already had occasion to consider. Undoubtedly prayer was no mere brief or perfunctory part of early Christian worship, but a considerable part of it, and this included preformed prayers like the Lord's Prayer and this prayer said after the Lord's Supper. This should not surprise us, since synagogue worship followed a liturgy. All was not spontaneous and pneumatic in early Christian worship, at least not in Jewish Christian circles.

IN THIS CHAPTER we have looked at some length at praise and prayer, at song and supplication, trying to get a better glimpse of what early Christian worship would have looked like. We could as well spend a good deal of time examining how Christians continued the Jewish tradition of almsgiving as part of worship, moving from James's request to Paul to remember the poor (Gal. 2:10), to Paul's pursuing the collection for the saints in Jerusalem (see, e.g., 2 Cor. 8–9), to the summaries in Acts 2 and 4 and the discussion about Ananias and Sapphira and Barnabas in Acts 4–5, as well as many other passages. Undoubtedly, prayer, praise, and almsgiving, all done in the synagogue, continued in the church, but what about the reading of Scripture and its exposition followed by exhortation? Was there preaching in the early Christian worship service by gifted preachers? The answer to this question is yes, and we must consider some of the homiletical material we find in the New Testament in our next chapter.

Questions for Reflection and Discussion

1. How does or how should the Holy Spirit's presence in the church change the character of worship?
2. What do you think Paul means when he talks about singing songs "in the Spirit"? What's the difference between enthusiastic singing and Spirit-inspired singing? Paul mentions hymns, psalms, and spiritual songs. Why are different sorts of songs important, especially for different types of services?
3. What is it about worship that could lead to parallel exhortations that include not only singing but also submitting to one another in love?
4. What do you make of the fact that the original early Christian hymns had such deep theological content, and specifically Christological content? What does this tell us about some modern Christian songs that have little such content?
5. The evidence strongly suggests that early Christian worship involved prayers (including the Lord's Prayer), creedal statements, confessions, singing, preaching, teaching, and the expression of spiritual gifts, including prophecy and even speaking in tongues. Do you think these things should all be part and parcel of worship today? Why or why not?
6. What role should the Lord's Supper and baptism play in Christian worship? How regularly should communion be offered as a part of Christian worship? Why should these worship acts be seen as sacraments, as means of grace?

CHAPTER SIX

Illuminating the Good News

He was a preacher, too . . . and never charged nothing for his preaching, and it was worth it, too.

Mark Twain

Society can overlook murder, adultery, or swindling; it never forgives preaching of a new gospel.

Edmund Burke

The Church is the Church in her worship. Worship is not an optional extra, but is of the very life and essence of the Church. . . . Man is never more truly man than when he worships God. He rises to all the heights of human dignity when he worships God, and all God's purposes in Creation and in Redemption are fulfilled in us as together in worship we are renewed in and through Christ, and in the name of Christ we glorify God.

James B. Torrance, "The Place of Jesus Christ in Worship"

We have already noticed that Christian preaching in house churches by Paul and others could be lengthy (Acts 20:7). This was not just evangelistic preaching, but preaching to those who were already disciples. And sometimes there would be special preaching occasions when one leader would need to preach to others, as Paul does in Acts 20:13-37. Here he exhorts the Ephesian elders, drawing on the Old Testament, the teaching of Jesus, and the apostolic tradition that he and others had generated. Interestingly enough, Acts 20:13-37 is the only full-dress sermon to Christians that we have from Paul in Acts, doubtless because it is a book about missionary efforts — but then Paul's letters are replete with such preaching materials.

I would suggest, in fact, that often what we are looking at in the so-called New Testament letters are actually homilies, sermons, and rhetorical discourses meant to be delivered in worship settings by whatever co-worker was able to take the document and effectively and persuasively communicate it in person. However, since some *still* haven't gotten the memo on the oral and rhetorical character of the New Testament world, it will be helpful for me to make some general remarks about that first, before we consider a brief sampling of early Christian homiletics.[1]

The Oral and Rhetorical World of the Apostles

Ours is a text-based culture, a culture of written documents. You need look no further than your computer screens to verify this assertion. We live in an Internet age only because there's widespread literacy, which in turn leads to the widespread production and reading of texts. It is thus difficult for us to conceive of and understand the character of an oral culture, much less understand how sacred texts function in such a culture. Yet, however difficult, it is important that we try to understand such a thing, since all of the cultures of the Bible were essentially oral cultures, not text-based

1. This discussion can be found in a much fuller form in my book *What's in the Word* (Waco, Tex.: Baylor University Press, 2009).

cultures, and their texts were in fact oral texts. That might sound like an oxymoron, but in fact it is not.

The literacy rate in the cultures of the New Testament era seems to have ranged from about 5 percent to 20 percent, depending on the culture and the subgroup within the culture. Not surprisingly, then, all ancient peoples, whether literate or not, preferred the living word, which is to say the spoken word. Texts were enormously expensive to produce: papyrus was costly, ink was costly, and scribes were extremely costly. Being a secretary in Jesus' or Paul's age could be a lucrative job indeed. No wonder Jesus said to his audiences, "Let those who have ears, listen." Notice that he never said, "Let those who have eyes, read." Most eyes in the New Testament period could not read.

So far as we can tell, no documents in antiquity were intended for "silent" reading, and only a few were intended for private individuals to read. They were always meant to be read out loud and usually read out loud to a group of people. For the most part they were simply necessary surrogates for oral communication. This was particularly true of ancient letters.

In fact, most ancient documents, including letters, were not really texts at all in the modern sense. They were composed with their aural and oral potential in mind, and they were meant to be orally delivered when they arrived at their destination. Thus, for example, when one reads the opening verses of Ephesians in the original Greek, loaded as they are with aural devices (assonance, alliteration, rhythm, rhyme, various rhetorical devices), it becomes perfectly clear that no one was ever meant to hear this in any language but Greek, and furthermore, no one was ever meant to read this silently. It needed to be heard in Greek.

And indeed there was a third reason a document needed to be orally delivered. Because of the cost of making documents, a standard letter in Greek would be written in all capital letters and have no separation of words, sentences, paragraphs, and the like, and little or no punctuation. Imagine having to sort out a document that began as follows:

PAULASERVANTOFCHRISTJESUSCALLEDTOBEANAPOST
LEANDSETAPARTFORTHEGOSPELOFGOD.

The only way to decipher such a collection of letters was to sound
them out — out loud! There is, of course, the famous anecdote
about St. Augustine and St. Ambrose. Augustine said that Ambrose was the most remarkable man he had ever met, because he
could read without moving his lips or making a sound. Clearly, an
oral culture is a different world than a largely literate, text-based
culture, and texts function differently in such a world. All sorts of
texts were simply surrogates for oral speech, and this statement
applies to most of the biblical texts themselves.[2]

It is hard for us to wrap our minds around it, but texts were
scarce in the biblical world and often were treated with great respect. Because literacy was largely a skill that only the educated
possessed, and because the educated tended to be almost exclu-
sively from the social elite, texts in such a world served the purpose of the elite: conveying their authority, passing down their
judgments, establishing their property claims, indicating their he-
redity, and the like. But since all ancient people were profoundly
religious, the most important documents even among the elite
were religious texts, sacred texts.

What do texts in an oral culture tell us about their authors? It
is too seldom taken into account that the twenty-seven books of
the New Testament reflect a remarkable level of literacy and indeed of rhetorical skill among the inner circle of leaders of the
early Christian movement. Early Christianity was not, by and
large, a movement led by illiterate peasants or the socially de-
prived. For the most part, the leaders of the movement produced
the texts of the movement, and the texts of the New Testament re-

2. On levels of literacy and the creation of ancient texts, see Harry Y. Gamble, *Books and Readers in the Early Church: A History of Early Christian Texts*
(New Haven: Yale University Press, 1995), pp. 1-41.

flect a considerable knowledge of Greek, of rhetoric, and indeed of general Greco-Roman culture. This skill and erudition can only seldom be attributed to scribes, except in cases where scribes such as Tertius or Sosthenes (see Rom. 16 and 1 Cor. 1) had been converted and had donated their skills to the movement. Even then, however, it appears that they were largely just taking dictation from Paul. Most of the letters we find in the New Testament are far longer than secular letters of their era.

Actually *they are not letters for the most part,* though they sometimes have epistolary openings and closings. They are in fact discourses, homilies, and rhetorical speeches of various sorts which the creators could not deliver in person to a particular audience, and so instead they sent a surrogate to proclaim them. These documents would not be handed to just anyone. From what we can tell, Paul expected one of his co-workers such as Timothy or Titus or Phoebe to undertake the task of orally delivering the contents of such documents in a rhetorically effective manner. This almost certainly would have been a necessity, since every document would come without punctuation or division of words, so only someone skilled in reading such "seamless prose" — and indeed, one who *already knew* the contents of the document — could place the emphases in the right places so as to effectively communicate the message.

Some New Testament scholars have suggested that Christians only used some sort of unique literary genre in telling the Gospel story, or that their preaching was unlike proclamation on other subjects in the Empire. This actually is false. Averil Cameron puts it this way:

A few New Testament critics, taking "new" in its most literal sense, have made extravagant claims: "a new speech from new depths"; "the miraculous unedited newness of the word." Yet this "new" Christianity was able to develop a means to ensure its place as a rival to and then inheritor of the old elite culture. . . . Christian discourse too made its way in the wider world less by revolutionary novelty than by the procedure of working through the familiar, by appealing from the known to the unknown.[3]

Cameron goes on to add, "Early Christian rhetoric was not always, I shall argue, the specialized discourse its own practitioners often claimed it to be. Consequently, its reception was easier and wider ranging than modern historians allow, and its effects correspondingly more telling. The seemingly alternative rhetorics, the classical or pagan and the Christian, were more nearly one than their respective practitioners, interested in scoring off each other, would have us believe."[4]

How, then, did a sacred text function in an oral and rhetorical culture? For one thing, it was believed that words, especially religious words, were not mere ciphers or symbols. They were believed to have power and to affect people if they were properly communicated and pronounced. It was not just the sacred names of God, the so-called *nomina sacra,* which were considered to have inherent power, but sacred words in general. Consider, for example, what Isaiah 55:11 says: "So shall my word be that goes forth out of my mouth: it shall not return to me void, but it shall accomplish that which I please, and it shall prosper in the thing I sent it to do." The Word or words of a living and powerful God were viewed as living and powerful in themselves.[5] Thus we can imagine how a precious and expensive document which contained God's *own* words would be viewed. It would be something that needed to be kept in a sacred place, like a temple or a synagogue, and only certain persons, with clean hands and pure hearts, would

---

3. Averil Cameron, *Christianity and the Rhetoric of Empire* (Berkeley and Los Angeles: University of California Press, 1991), pp. 24-25.

4. Cameron, *Christianity and the Rhetoric of Empire,* p. 20.

5. See my little book *The Living Word of God* (Waco, Tex.: Baylor University Press, 2007).

be allowed to unroll the sacred scroll and read it, much less interpret it.

From what we can tell, the texts of the New Testament books were treasured during the first century and were lovingly and carefully copied for centuries thereafter. There is even evidence, beginning in the second century, of the use of female Christian scribes, who had a "fairer" hand, to copy and even begin to deco rate these sacred texts.[6] But make no mistake — even such texts were seen as serving the largely oral culture. Before the rise of modern education and widespread literacy, it had always been true that "In the beginning was the (spoken) Word."[7] All of this has implications for how we should approach the New Testament, especially the more ad hoc documents in the Pauline corpus, and the other documents traditionally called letters in the New Testament, which sometimes, in fact, are not letters at all. First John is a sermon with neither epistolary opening nor closing. Hebrews is an even longer sermon, with only an epistolary closing, but of course no listener would ever have considered it a letter on first hearing, because there were no signals at the outset of the document to suggest such a thing. And in an oral culture, opening signals are everything if the question is "What sort of discourse or document am I listening to?" This is why Luke 1:1-4 is so crucial to judging the genre of that Gospel.

Given that the distinction between a speech and an orally performed text was more like a thin veil than a thick wall between literary categories, it will come as no surprise when I say that oral conventions actually shape more of the so-called epistolary litera-

---

6. See K. Haines-Eitzen, *Guardians of Letters* (Oxford: Oxford University Press, 2000).

7. It is interesting that an important literate figure like Papias of Hierapolis, who lived at the end of the New Testament era, repeatedly said that he preferred the living voice of the apostle or one who had heard the eyewitnesses to a written document. In this he simply reflected the typical attitude of ancient peoples, literate or not.

We Have Seen His Glory

ture of the New Testament than epistolary conventions, and with good reason. This is so not only because of the dominant oral character of the culture, but also, and more importantly, because the Greco-Roman world of the New Testament period was a rhetorically saturated environment, whereas the influence of literacy and letters was far less widespread so far as we can tell. Thus, we need to understand an important fact: The rise to prominence of the personal letter used as a vehicle for instruction or as a treatise of sorts was a phenomenon which only really took root in the Greco-Roman milieu with the letters of Cicero shortly before the New Testament era. And we need to contrast this with the long history of the use of rhetoric going back to Aristotle, and the use of it in numerous different venues.

Rhetoric was a tool useable with the educated and the uneducated, with the elite and with the ordinary, and most public speakers of any ilk or skill in antiquity knew they had to use the art of persuasion to accomplish their aims. Not only were there schools of rhetoric throughout the Mediterranean crescent, but rhetoric itself was part of elementary education as well as secondary and tertiary education. There were no comparable schools of letter-writing, not least because it was a rather recent art just coming to prominence in the first century A.D. And here we come to a crucial point.

Analyzing the majority of the New Testament on the basis of epistolary conventions can be a helpful exercise to some degree. But since many of these did not become de rigeur and were not put into a handbook until *after* New Testament times, they cannot constitute the dominant literary paradigm by which we examine the Pauline, Petrine, Johannine, and other discourses in the New Testament. When it came to words and the conveying of ideas, meaning, and persuasion in the New Testament era, the dominant paradigm was rhetoric, not epistolary conventions.

This is why I will say now that most of the New Testament owes far more to rhetoric and its very long-standing and widespread conventions than to the relatively nascent practice of writing letter-essays or letter treatises. Most of the letters of the New Testament, with the exception of the very shortest ones (2 John, 3 John, perhaps Philemon), look very little like the very mundane and pragmatic epistolary literature of that era. In terms of both structure and content, most New Testament documents look far more like rhetorical speeches. Some are in fact "words of exhortation," as the author of Hebrews calls his homily; some are more rhetorical speeches suitable for assemblies where discussion would then ensue (e.g., after-dinner discussion at a symposium). But all are profitably analyzed in detail by means of rhetorical examination.

Thus, for example, the beginning and end of Paul's letters almost always reflect epistolary conventions, and the documents themselves can certainly be categorized as a form of ancient letters. But these epistolary categories help us very little in analyzing the structure of the material if we're not dealing with the epistolary opening and closing elements (prescript, travel plans, opening or closing greetings). Furthermore, there was no convention of placing a "thanksgiving prayer" at the outset of an ancient letter or a doxology at the end, nor are we helped by lumping the vast majority of a discourse under the heading of "body middle." This really tells us nothing about the document, and it wasn't an ancient epistolary category in any case.

To reiterate, epistolary conventions and devices help us very little with the bulk of the material in the documents traditionally called New Testament letters. Here is where rhetoric has proved much more helpful in unlocking the structural and substantive intricacies of the majority of New Testament documents. Even Paul's letters were not meant to be privately studied. In the first instance, they were surrogates for the speeches Paul would have made could he have been present with his audience. And as such they partake of all the ad-hoc characteristics of such purpose-driven ancient speeches. They were intended as timely remarks, their goal being to affect the belief and the behavior of the various audiences. They were not intended merely as theological or ethical treatises. Rhetorical criticism helps us realize the dynamic, interactive, and homiletical nature of these documents.

At this juncture I want to offer a few examples of the helpfulness of rhetorical analysis of the New Testament using the ancient categories of Greco-Roman rhetoric. In the first place, recognizing the rhetorical species of a document will explain much about its content and its intent. For example, Ephesians is an epideictic homily (that is, designed primarily for the rhetoric of praise and blame) written not to a specific situation but to a series of Pauline churches, and it focuses on the rhetoric of praise — in particular, praise of Christ, the church, and the unity between them and among them.[8] No thesis statement or "proposition" is required in epideictic rhetoric, nor are finely honed arguments proving a case necessary. Rather, the intention is to get the audience caught up in wonder and love and praise of someone or some subject. In 1 John, which reflects no epistolary features at all and should never have been called a letter, we have a beautiful epideictic homily about love and the character of God and the Christian life, where virtues are praised and vices are discouraged.

Failure to recognize the rhetorical signals in numerous New Testament documents like those mentioned has led to many false conclusions, especially when it comes to the letters and homilies of the New Testament. It is safe to say that rhetorical criticism of the New Testament has established itself as a viable and vital means of analysis in the last twenty-five years, and promises to yield yet more fruit in the years to come.[9]

The good news about this approach is that it is not merely modern; it is also ancient. It was used by many of the great com-

8. See the discussion in Witherington, *The Letters to Philemon, the Colossians, and the Ephesians* (Grand Rapids: Wm. B. Eerdmans, 2007).

9. For an introductory textbook on the subject, see Witherington, *New Testament Rhetoric* (Eugene, Ore.: Cascade Books, 2008).

mentators on the Greek New Testament through the ages, ranging from John Chrysostom to Melanchthon and beyond. It thus has a long and noble pedigree. In my view, it is time for a paradigm shift. The New Testament documents we have been discussing should in the first instance be analyzed primarily by ancient social and rhetorical conventions, and only secondarily by epistolary ones. In this way we will put the emphasis on the right syllable and analyze the documents primarily in the way that first-century readers or hearers would have.

I want to return just briefly to the issue of the function of sacred texts in particular in an oral and rhetorical culture. I cannot emphasize enough how the living voice was preferred to its literary residue if the speech was taken down or written out beforehand. Rhetoric, thank goodness, attended not just to logic and issues of content but to such things as gestures, tone of voice, speed of delivery, and the like, for we are talking about the ancient art of homiletics. Rather than form following function, function dictated form.

This was all the more the case when it came to the proclamation of a profoundly religious message, especially one based on one or more sacred texts. Sacred texts had an aura, a presence, a palpable character as the embodiment of the voice of a living god. That voice was considered powerful indeed. Ancient peoples would write out their curses on lead foil, roll them up, and place them near or under the altar in a temple, believing that the breath of the deity would animate and act out those words, because the word of a god was a speech-act indeed, an active word that changed things and affected persons, that could serve as either blessing or curse, boon or bane. In this light, let us hear a brief passage from one of Paul's letters, which most scholars think is our very earliest New Testament document: 1 Thessalonians. In the second chapter, verse 13 reads as follows: "And we also thank God continually because when you received the word of God, which you heard from us, you accepted it, not as a human word, but as it actually is, the word of God, which is at work in you who believe."[10]

I will resist the temptation to preach at this juncture, but here is a text that cries out for adequate exposition. First, we note that Paul refers to his own proclamation of the Gospel to the Thessalonians as "the word of God." Paul has no doubt that he's speaking God's very word to them, and you'll notice that he's not referring to pre-existing sacred texts from the Old Testament. No, he's talking about the message conveyed about Jesus. Second, we notice that he says that this preaching was by no means only, or even mainly, his own words, or the words of human beings or human wisdom. Indeed, it really was God's living word. Notice, however, that he uses the singular. The phrase is "the word of God," which reminds us of previous things that could be called "the word of God," ranging from the utterances of the Old Testament prophets to the sacred texts of the Old Testament themselves. But primacy here is given to the spoken word of God, not to something written — a "Good News" word of God.

Third, Paul says that this word of God (singular) had lodged in the lives of the Thessalonians and that it was "still at work in you who believe." This word of God had taken up residence in the Thessalonian converts and was doing soul work in and on them. It was a living and active two-edged sword penetrating their very being, just as the author of Hebrews was to suggest in 4:12-13, and he too wasn't talking about a text; he was talking about an oral proclamation which penetrates the heart. If we ask the question "Did any of the New Testament writers believe they were writing sacred, God-breathed texts?" it seems to me that the answer must surely be yes — first of all because someone like Paul believed that he was speaking the very word of God to his converts, not merely his own words or opinions, and furthermore because he saw his

10. See the more detailed explanation in Witherington, *The Letters to the Thessalonians* (Grand Rapids: Wm. B. Eerdmans, 2005).

letters as just the surrogate for a speech he would have given in person had he been there.

It is no mere rhetoric, full of sound and fury but signifying little, to say that analyzing the New Testament orally and rhetorically gets us back in touch with the original ethos and character of these oral texts and better prepares us for understanding their homiletical functions in early Christian worship. What we need to do at this juncture is some brief sampling from three early Christian sermons: Hebrews, 1 John, and James.

The Preaching of Early Christian Orators

From what little we can discern, early Jewish homilies tended to be largely exhortations, or, put another way, ethically focused.[11] The earliest clues we have on the matter of synagogue worship come from Alexandria and Philo (*Legum Allegoriae*, 3.162-68, and his *De Mutatione Nominum*, 253-63), and what he tells us indeed suggests a less formal institution which met sometimes in homes and sometimes in purpose-built structures. They met for prayer and what we might call Bible and religious study — an early version of Hebrew school — and some form of worship on Shabbat (Friday evening). Later Talmudic evidence about a lectionary cycle of readings, sometimes anachronistically projected back into the first century, probably is not that relevant. But what we can say is that there is clear evidence that the Torah was read in the worship service and was expounded upon in some form.[12]

We may think of the brief synopsis offered by Luke in Luke 4:16-27, which may provide us with some clues. There we have

---

11. See the introduction in Witherington, *Letters and Homilies for Jewish Christians* (Downers Grove, Ill.: InterVarsity Press, 2007).

12. See L. I. Levine, "The Nature and Origin of the Palestinian Synagogue Reconsidered," *Journal of Biblical Literature* 115 (1996): 425-48; here pp. 431-32, 439-41.

reading of Scripture, exposition of a sort, and exhortation in answer to the response of the audience. This experience seems to have had an interactive dimension. Questions could be put to the speaker, and he would answer, perhaps after the initial exposition. We know that there were early rules of exegesis laid down by Hillel in the first century (the so-called Seven Rules). One would comment on a particular text, then relate it to other texts, sometimes in a sort of chain reference or catena-like citation (cf. Philo, *De Specialibus Legibus*, 2.15, no. 62; *Quod Omnis Probus Liber Sit*, 12, no. 81-82).[13]

It comes as no surprise, then, that a number of the homilies in the New Testament written by Jewish Christians are mostly ethically or practically focused — for example, James and 1 John. To be sure, Hebrews has a good deal more theological reflection, but at the end of the day, the author calls his sermon a "word of exhortation" (Heb. 13:22), the very same language applied to the synagogue sermon in Acts 13:15. Apparently, behavior and praxis were the main emphases in synagogue messages.

As I have shown at length elsewhere, the theology in Hebrews serves, undergirds, and drives the exhortations in this particular sermon as the author toggles back and forth between theological exposition of texts and exhortations throughout Hebrews 1–13. No listening audience would ever have guessed that Hebrews was a letter from the beginning of the sermon, which has no epistolary elements whatsoever.

Compare this to the homily we call James, which is a circular sermon on how to live wisely and well, and does have a bit of an epistolary element (addresser, addressee) at the outset, rather like Ephesians, which is the same sort of circular sermon sent from a distance. First John has no epistolary elements whatsoever, being

13. See the discussion of P. H. Davids, "Homily, Ancient," in *Dictionary of New Testament Background*, ed. C. A. Evans and S. E. Porter (Downers Grove, Ill.: InterVarsity Press, 2000), pp. 515-18, especially pp. 515-16.

an ethical homily on core values and qualities and behaviors that the author wants to reinforce in his audience's lives. The upshot of what I have just said is that in the documents most obviously categorized as sermons in the New Testament (Hebrews, 1 John, James — all written by Jewish Christians), the majority of the material in them is ethically driven or simply exhortative in intent and character. Briefly considering some of what's going on in these homilies will tell us a good deal about the worship life of the house church. Let's start with the longest of these documents first: Hebrews.

Hebrews

D. J. Harrington has called Hebrews "arguably the greatest Christian sermon ever written down,"[14] high praise for a sermon that is anonymous and got into the canon by being (wrongly) associated with the Pauline corpus. The reason for the anonymity is not because the preacher was shy, but because sermons didn't tend to need signatures, as the audiences already knew who had produced them. The homiletical character of Hebrews and 1 John explains the anonymity and reflects this intimate connection between proclaimer and audience. Thomas Long, himself a homiletician, has characterized Hebrews as follows:

> Hebrews, like all good sermons, is a dialogical event in a monological format. The Preacher does not hurl information and arguments at the readers as if they were targets. Rather, Hebrews is written to create a conversation, to evoke participation, to prod the faithful memories of the readers. Beginning with the first sentence, "us" and "we" language abounds. Also,

14. D. J. Harrington, *What Are They Saying about The Letter to the Hebrews?* (Mahwah, N.J.: Paulist Press, 2005), p. 1.

We Have Seen His Glory

the Preacher employs rhetorical questions to awaken the voice of the listener (see 1:5 and 1:14, for example); raps on the pulpit a bit when the going gets sluggish (5:11); occasionally restates the main point to insure that even the inattentive and drowsy are on board (see 8:1); doesn't bother to "footnote" the sources the hearers already know quite well (see the familiar preacher's phrase in 2:6: "Someone has said somewhere . . ."); and keeps making explicit verbal contact with the listeners (see 3:12 and 6:9, for example) to remind them that they are not only supposed to be listening to this sermon; they are also, by their active hearing, to be a part of creating it. As soon as [they] experience the rise and fall of the opening words of Hebrews, [readers become] aware that they are not simply watching a roller coaster hurtle along the rhetorical tracks; they are in the lead car. In Hebrews, the gospel is not merely an idea submitted for intellectual consideration; it is a life-embracing demand that summons to action.[15]

Depending on how one counts a quotation, there are about thirty quotations of the Old Testament in this discourse (not all of equal importance); there are also between thirty-five and forty allusions to texts from the Greek Old Testament. I use the term "Greek Old Testament" advisedly, because it is clear that sometimes our author is following the LXX (see Heb. 10:5, where Ps. 40:6 is cited, with the reading "body" instead of "ears," and Heb. 11:21, citing Gen. 47:31, with the reading "staff" instead of "bed," as in the Hebrew). However, sometimes he follows a text of the Greek Old Testament which does not conform to what we know of the LXX readings. What we can say with some assurance, however, is that our author is not following the Hebrew text and simply translating it in these other cases (see, e.g., the citation of Jer. 31:33-34 at Heb. 8:10-12 and 10:16-17). Sometimes our author may

15. Thomas Long, *Hebrews* (Louisville: John Knox Press, 1997), p. 6.

just be paraphrasing or citing from memory (see Ps. 22:22 at Heb. 2:12 or Ps. 95:7-11 cited at Heb. 3:9-10). His use of the Old Testament is complex, and most frequently Christological and typological in character.[16] It is quite evident that our author is saturated in the LXX.

In about twenty of the direct quotations of the Old Testament in Hebrews, God is the grammatical subject, such that God speaks directly to the audience of this discourse. Clearly our author believes that the Old Testament is God's living Word, which still speaks authoritatively, even to an audience now under a new and different covenant. In fact, we have the phrases "God says," "Christ says," and the "Holy Spirit says" (all present tense), which introduce Old Testament quotations. But we need not think that our author is cavalier in his use of the Old Testament. Fred Craddock rightly urges, "The writer of the epistle does not, in an act of interpretive tyranny, simply make irresponsible raids on the Old Testament to construct his own theological house, leaving among his scriptural sources not one stone upon another. Hebrews is not only the most extended treatment of the Old Testament in the New, but it is also, along with Luke, the most respectful of continuity. The Bible tells one story, not two, and it is the story of God's saving initiative toward humankind."[17] What we also need to say is that our author is doing his best to make the Old Testament serviceable for Christian worship and education by showing how it is indeed meant for his audience and will lead them to remain Christians, not return to simply being non-Christian Jews.

The hermeneutical perspective of our author is intimated and in some respects even indicated in the first two verses of the Prologue: "Partial and piecemeal in the past God spoke to our ances-

16. See the discussion by H. Attridge, "Hebrews, Epistle to the," in *The Anchor Bible Dictionary*, vol. 3, ed. D. N. Freedman (New York: Doubleday, 1992), pp. 97-105; here p. 102.

17. Fred Craddock, "The Letter to the Hebrews," in *The New Interpreter's Bible*, vol. 12 (Nashville: Abingdon, 1998), p. 13.

We Have Seen His Glory

tors through the prophets; at the end of these days he spoke to us in the Son."[18] Our author writes with an eschatological perspective, believing that God's climactic and indeed perfect speaking and self-revelation have come in the Son, after partially revealing himself through the prophets in the past:

> There is certainly a conception of a longitudinal "revelation history," in which earlier and more fragmentary forms of God's Address have been overtaken and replaced by a perfected form of the same thing. There is thus established between the various moments of the revelation history a recognizable continuity which allows them, in spite of their discontinuity, to be construed as parts of a single process. . . . This means that it is the Speaking of God itself which contains the real continuity and which allows the historical (or empirical) forms which it takes to itself be recognizably moments in an ongoing process. But there is also a strong *dis*continuity insofar as the perfected form of this speaking stands over against the preliminary forms. As the goal, or the end term, of any process of development is recognizably something different from the process itself . . . so the Word in the Son stands over against the Word in the prophets. The process *has* reached its end term and has therefore achieved perfection because the Word in the Son is the eschatological form of what God has to say. The Son, as the bearer of the perfected form of God's Address, accordingly stands — as their fulfillment — over against the earlier, anticipatory forms mediated through the prophets.[19]

One of the things that follows from this historical and eschatological perspective is that Old Testament figures and institutions exist as ante-types and foreshadowings of Christ and vari-

18. Graham Hughes, *Hebrews and Hermeneutics* (Cambridge: Cambridge University Press, 1979), p. 6.

19. Hughes, *Hebrews and Hermeneutics,* p. 6.

ous aspects of his life and work. The preliminary revelation is re-interpreted in light of its eschatological goal; it is not suggested that the final revelation is merely the completion of a long process, or that the new covenant is just the final form of the old, or that Jesus is Melchizedek redivivus, or that the events of the eschatological age are just fulfillments of Old Testament prophecy. All of this becomes especially clear when our author interprets a whole series of Old Testament passages in light of the Christ event, past and present, many of which were not messianic prophecies to begin with. Since preaching was an essential element in Jewish and early Christian worship, it became critical that orators and writers like the author of Hebrews be able to demonstrate at length how the Torah could in fact be used in and for Christian worship. Our author's view is that all along the Torah was intended especially for Christians and their worship.

Promise/fulfillment is not all there is to our author's hermeneutic. That the Old Testament still has meaning and still speaks does not mean that the covenant it speaks mainly of — namely, the Mosaic covenant — is still deemed valid or binding. The issue is not meaning or even truth or revelation. Our author believes that all of the Old Testament still has meaning and truth and is a revelation from God. And of course the Old Testament takes on more meaning, not less, when interpreted through a Christological lens. The hermeneutical issue is applicability now that the Christ has come and the new covenant and the new age have been inaugurated. Our author sees the former covenant as obsolete and therefore inapplicable, even for Jewish Christians. They may and must learn from it. They are not obligated to keep it. Yet at the same time, the Old Testament is still the living word of God for the audience, and I am sure that our author would have happily endorsed the glowing statement about the Old Testament and its usefulness for Christians found in 2 Timothy 3:16.

What we are able to say here is that since this homily is meant to be heard in the context of worship, we should evaluate it in that light. In worship we praise God for what he has done and is, and draw near to him as the letter exhorts us to do, but in worship we also hear and learn what we must go forth and do. Hebrews, then, is a vehicle for worship that leads to the right sort of service. The progression may be seen as follows: "Since we have [indicative] . . . let us draw near [imperative based on indicative] . . . so we may hold fast [possibility created by the first two steps]." What believers have provides the basis for and enables their response. The point is that now believers are better equipped to respond, since the final work of God through Christ has already come to pass. The work of God has effected what believers are, and therefore has enabled them to do what they must do.

A. T. Lincoln suggests that our author believes that the Old Testament provides the following for the Christian: (1) it provides aspirations which only Christ can fulfill; (2) it offers a vision of our *telos* and perfection — that is, we are to have dominion over the cosmos, and already have it in Christ; (3) it offers a dream of the day when we cease from our labors and enter into God's rest; (4) it offers a desire to be free of sin's stain, and a recognition that sin against God and fellow humans is the essential human problem; (5) it offers a longing for free access to the divine presence; (6) it provides picture language — shadows and copies to prepare for the coming of Christ and God's final word; and (7) in Melchizedek it provides a partial anticipation of the eternal priest and new covenant. To this we may add that it offers paraenesis (exhortation), which our author sees as often just as applicable to his own audience as to the Old Testament ones.[20]

But is there some rhetorical logic to the alternations between exposition and exhortation in this homily? The answer is yes, and has been rightly discerned by T. W. Seid. What he points out is

20. I was fortunate enough to have A. T. Lincoln as my instructor in the exegesis of Hebrews in seminary, and at various junctures this section is indebted to his many insights, most of which have, sadly, never been published.

that the expositions are part of a larger effort to draw comparisons principally between Christ and others. Thus, he sees the structure here as follows: comparison of Son and angels (1:1-14) and paraenesis (2:1-18); comparison of Moses and Christ (3:1-6) and paraenesis (3:7–4:16); comparison of Aaron and Christ (5:1-10) and paraenesis (5:11–6:20); comparison of Melchizedek/Christ and the Levitical priesthood (7:1-25) and paraenesis (7:26–8:3); comparison of the first covenant and the new covenant (8:4–10:18) and paraenesis (10:19–12:29); and epistolary appendix (13:1-25). This *synkrisis*/paraenesis alternation[21] encourages the audience to progress in moral conduct by remaining faithful to the greater revelation in Jesus Christ and emulating the models of its scripture; it also warns the audience of the greater judgment to befall those unfaithful to the greater revelation.[22]

What is praised and what is blamed in this discourse is not part of some abstruse exercise in exegesis for its own sake. It is part of a pastoral effort to deal with the struggles the Jewish Christians were having in Rome to remain true and faithful to the things they had already committed themselves to embrace. To this end, our author's rhetorical strategy in choosing the texts that he does has nothing to do with his intellectual curiosity about messianism or a Christological reading of the Old Testament. Rather, Psalms 8, 95, 110 (and perhaps 40), Jeremiah 31, Habakkuk 2, and Proverbs 3 are texts which he chose and dealt with because they help make the case that the inadequacy or ineffectiveness or "partial and piecemeal" character of previous revelation and covenants is self-attested in the Old Testament.[23] But that is only the negative side of

---

21. A *synkrisis* is a rhetorical comparison in which two persons or things or events are compared in order to highlight or lift up the one over the other, even if they are both viewed positively.

22. See T. W. Seid, "The Rhetorical Form of the Melchizedek/Christ Comparison in Hebrews 7," Ph.D. diss., Brown University, 1996.

23. G. B. Caird, "The Exegetical Method of the Epistle to the Hebrews," *Canadian Journal of Theology* 5 (1959): 44-51.

the persuasion going on in this rhetorical masterpiece, with its carefully selected, inartificial proofs from the Old Testament.

Our author brings in other texts as well to support the positive side of the argument, which is that the good things which the Old Testament said were yet to come are now realized only in Christ, and faithfulness is required if these eschatological promises are to be realized also in the lives of those who follow Christ. Thus it can be said that "theology is the handmaiden of paraenesis in this 'word of exhortation,' as the author himself describes it."[24] The author is not merely "preaching for a verdict"; he is preaching to avert defection in his audience, and this required a strong focus on exhortation, undergirded with the theology necessary to sustain it. In this brilliant homily our author intends to reinforce things that his audience has already embraced but is now struggling with. Something similar seems to be going on in 1 John.

First John

Philo, speaking of students at a Sabbath school in Alexandria, explains what they were taught: "They were trained in piety, holiness, justice, domestic and civic conduct, knowledge of what is truly good or evil, or indifferent, and how to choose what they should do and avoid the opposite, taking for their defining standards these three — love of God, love of virtue, love of people" (*Every Good Man Is Free,* 83).

What is striking to me about this brief summary is how well it comports with the character and content of 1 John, which is all about distinguishing good and evil and about love of God and

---

24. J. Walters, "The Rhetorical Arrangement of Hebrews," *Asbury Theological Journal* 51 (1996): 59-70; here p. 63. Here I have been following and am indebted to Walters' compelling argument.

each other — with, of course, the additional important element of Christology. Two other points are germane here. We should stress the ethical or paraenetic aim of most early Jewish preaching, such that it could be characterized as a "word of exhortation," as well as the influence of rhetoric on early Jewish preaching in the first century A.D., particularly outside of the Holy Land. The Christological or doctrinal sort of beginning to 1 John and the continuing reminders about the correct Christological beliefs shouldn't fool us into thinking that 1 John is primarily or essentially a theological tract. The theology is introduced to undergird and guide the ethical response being prompted and urged in this discourse. The focus is actually more on behavior than on belief, though the latter is fundamental as well.

In addition to these basic observations, we may add the important observation that this homily is profoundly sapiential in character. It is a form of wisdom utterance, not unlike some of the exhortations we find in Proverbs or Ben Sira, with our author assuming the same sort of pedagogical posture as we find the sage assuming in Proverbs 1–7, where he speaks as a father to his spiritual children. As in this earlier Wisdom literature, in 1 John we will find a great deal of repetition and amplification of basic themes. The author will use much wordplay and rhetorical finesse as he makes his discourse both memorable and memorizable through the interlocking and intertwined use of polar-opposite key terms and phrases like "light and darkness," "sin and cleansing/sanctification," and "love and hate."

In a way this discourse is rather like a musical round, with the author offering us permutations and combinations of certain basic themes in order to reinforce understanding and insure the desired response. We might compare its effect to the similar sort of effect in Ecclesiastes. Finally, we must stress that the Christology which is manifested in this discourse is also a form of Wisdom Christology in which Wisdom has come in person — in this case in the flesh as Jesus to instruct and save his people — and we must listen for the echoes of what is said about Wisdom coming and attempting to rescue God's people found in Wisdom literature ranging from Proverbs to the Wisdom of Solomon to Ben Sira.[25]

Epideictic rhetoric is, by its very nature, repetitive and even hyperbolic, seeking to strengthen adherence to values already adopted or embraced by the audience, and also to draw out the implications of those values. This is quite clearly the rhetoric we have in the homily we call 1 John. We hear, for instance, that the author is writing to "you, fathers, because you have known . . . to you, young people, because you have overcome . . . to you, children, because you have known . . ." (1 John 2:13). He reminds them of the message they heard and have embraced from the beginning (1 John 3:11). He writes to those who already believe in the name of the Son of God (5:13). Epideictic rhetoric is, among other things, the rhetoric of funeral homilies, and in a sense our author is dealing with a postmortem situation. There has been a split in the Christian community, and some of its members have been lost because they have left the community. Healing is needed, reassurance must be offered, and reasons to continue to embrace the fundamental values must be given, because eternal life for the community's members hangs in the balance.

Epideictic rhetoric is also, by its very nature, highly emotive in character, for trust in the community's values and stronger adherence to them after a crisis require a deeper emotional commitment. It is not surprising that various commentators, sensing the emotive character of this homily, have assumed that we were dealing with polemics against the "Antichrists." And there is no doubt that our author is angry with those who have departed, more because they have committed apostasy than because they have left the community. While our author is prepared to say that they were never "of us," it is hard to doubt that the secessionists saw

25. See Witherington, *Jesus the Sage and the Pilgrimage of Wisdom* (Minneapolis: Fortress Press, 1994).

themselves as part of the community, and so may have seen themselves as followers of Christ in some sense, perhaps approving of some of his teachings.

The emotive language used of the departed (Antichrists, false prophets, and so on) is meant to help those remaining let them go and focus once more on their own spiritual well-being and belief system. It is meant to make sure that the community stops losing members and that none who remain are tempted to embrace the beliefs and behavior of the departed. This homily, then, is not about directly attacking or debating with opponents. It does not seek to delineate their views or refute them with detailed arguments. Our author assumes that the audience already knows the secessionists' views and feels it is sufficient to make a few salient points about their aberrant Christology, reiterating these points in various ways for emphasis and to insure agreement with them. Too much mirror-reading of 1 John has led to too much focus on the beliefs and behaviors of the departed and not enough on the beliefs and behaviors our author wants the audience to continue to embrace, an agenda furthered throughout this sermon.

Sermons were not uncommon in our author's time. They could be heard on a weekly basis in synagogues all across the Empire.[26] They were a particular sort of religious oration. Since Christian sermons, so far as we can tell, tended not to deal with priests, temples, and correct religious rituals (although some referred to circumcision or baptism, and some referred to the sacrifice of Christ), and since a good deal of the time they were not expositions of an Old Testament text, they would not generally have been viewed as specifically "religious" (as opposed to philosophical) in character by Gentiles who heard them.

In his first-rate study of the rhetoric of 1 John, Duane Watson shows in detail how 1 John uses amplification as one of its major

26. See Roy R. Jeal, *Integrating Theology and Ethics in Ephesians* (New York: Edwin Mellen Press, 2000), pp. 44-45.

rhetorical strategies.[27] Amplification is a rhetorical technique mainly associated with epideictic rhetoric and thus with sermons or homilies. Instead of offering a series of arguments proving a proposition or thesis statement, this sort of oration dedicates itself to amplifying and expanding and expounding on certain key ideas and themes which are already familiar and accepted (see Aristotle, *Rhetoric*, 1.9.1368a.38-40; Quintilian, *Institutio Oratoria*, 3.7.6). "The use of amplification," explains Watson, "indicates a careful working of the material and the need to be emphatic and clear in the face of the secessionist doctrine and practice to which [the author's] audience is subject. Far from being boringly *redundant*, the rhetoric is carefully *emphatic*."[28] The degree of emphatic repetition of key themes and ideas in 1 John shows just how concerned our author is about the need to strengthen the audience's embracing of these key values.

Our author uses a range of amplification techniques. He uses strong words such as *hate* and *murderers* (1 John 3:15). He also uses augmentation, a series of statements that increase in intensity, leading to a climax (e.g., 1 John 2:2: Jesus is an atoning sacrifice not only for the sins of the community but also for the sins of the whole world). Another device our author uses is the earlier-mentioned *synkrisis* or comparison (e.g., 1 John 5:9: Human testimony is good, but God's testimony is greater). In addition, he uses accumulation, the piling up of words or phrases identical in meaning or all referring to the same object or subject (e.g., 1 John 1:1-3: that which we have heard, seen, looked at, touched). Our author also uses a panoply of figures of repetition. One of these is *expolito*, which refers to the technique of saying the same thing with slight variation or with equivalent terms (*Her.,* 4.42.54). See, for example, 1 John 1:7b, 9b: "Cleansing us from all sin" later becomes "cleansing

27. Duane Watson, "Amplification Techniques in 1 John: The Interaction of Rhetorical Style and Invention," *Journal for the Study of the New Testament* 51 (1993): 99-123.

28. Watson, "Amplification Techniques in 1 John," pp. 122-23.

us from all unrighteousness." Another of these is *conduplicatio*, which refers to the repetition of the same word or the same phrase using the same part of speech, having the same function (1 John 2:12-14). Lest we mistake what's going on here, let me say that this doesn't indicate that our author has a very limited vocabulary. His repetition is a rhetorical strategy, a means of being emphatic.

Clearly the exigence or problem that prompted the writing of this homily was the schism that occurred (2:18-19), but this starting point doesn't reveal the character of the rhetoric here. What we find in this document is an attempt to increase the intensity of adherence to fundamental values already accepted, values which our sermonizer and his audience already hold in common, but which the audience may not see the full implications of. This is why we find the repeated use of the language of abiding (2:6, 10, 24, 28; 3:6, 24; 4:13, 16) and keeping (2:3-5; 3:22, 24).

Stephen Smalley has it essentially right when he says, "The purpose of 1 John may therefore be summarized as *primarily* an appeal to the faithful: to strengthen the faith and resolve of true believers in the Johannine community by encouraging them to maintain the apostolic Gospel."[29] In epideictic oratory, one tends to appeal to the most fundamental values and universal truths that the community adheres to, and in order to do that, our author has chosen to use sapiential language about love, light, life, truth, and the like, offering up sayings that in isolation would appear to be maxims or truisms to those who were already Christians. This is not the sort of discourse one uses when one's audience is not yet convinced of the truth of the Gospel.

Love; loyalty to the community; spiritual integrity and growth; avoiding false teaching and practices; maintaining the core values, including a profound commitment to Christ come in the flesh and his atoning sacrifice for sin; dealing with sin in one's own life; the older congregational members nurturing and

29. Stephen Smalley, *1, 2, 3 John* (Waco, Tex.: Word, 1984), p. xxviii.

We Have Seen His Glory

discipling the younger ones — these are some of the major themes our author wants to reinforce and amplify in this elegant and beguilingly simple sermon. But there is nothing mundane about it, because the author sees the embracing of these values as a matter of spiritual life and death.

James

Hebrews, while the grandest and fullest example in the canon of a Christian homily meant for Jewish Christians, is by no means the only one. Perhaps the oldest one we have is the so-called Letter of James, which in fact is really a sermon meant for all Jewish Christians outside the Holy Land. But James's modus operandi is very different indeed from that of the orator who wrote Hebrews. James, like his brother, is a sage, not, for the most part, an expositor of Old Testament texts. James offers new wisdom to his audience based on his own interpretations and expansions of some of Jesus' essential teachings. His concern is not with apostasy, which is the main concern in Hebrews, but rather with proper conduct in the community, including in the worship service. He focuses on concern for the poor, impartiality, prayer and healing, perseverance in the face of temptation, living according to the Law (in this case, the royal Law of Christ) — various of the usual concerns in Jewish life and, more particularly, synagogue life. Now let's take a more in-depth look at these concerns.

In James's 108 verses, there are about 59 imperatives, most of them in the second person (46), and ten are found in 4:7-10 alone, where the tone becomes strident.[30] What is notable about these imperatives is that usually they do not stand in isolation but are accompanied by explanations (using *hoti*: 1:12, 23; 2:10; 3:1; 4:3; 5:8,

30. See J. B. Polhill, "The Life Situation of the Book of James," *Review and Expositor* 66 (1969): 369-78.

11), warrants (using *gar:* 1:6, 7, 11, 13, 20, 24; 2:11, 13, 26; 3:2, 16; 4:14), or purpose clauses (1:3; 5:8). Notice as well that that there are clear signals that these imperatives do not stand alone but are part of a larger argument; this is shown by the use of *oun* ("so then" — 4:4, 7; 5:7, 16), *dio* ("therefore" — 1:21; 4:6), or even *houtos* ("and thus" — 1:11; 2:12, 17, 26; 3:5). Thus, while it is true that we have relatively few longer sentences (but see 2:2-4; 3:15-16; 4:13-15), it is important to realize that, by and large, what we do *not* have in this document is isolated exhortations. Instead, we have the sort of enthymematic argumentation — in shorthand, ethical arguments — that we also find in the Pastoral Epistles. An enthymeme is a syllogism with a missing member which the audience must supply to make sense of what is being said. Enthymematic rhetoric, therefore, demands audience participation. It is interesting that while our author is prepared to persuade, he is also not afraid to command, and he does so regularly as a part of the persuasion.

The question then becomes how proverbs, maxims, and various sorts of wisdom speech function in this sort of discourse. Generally speaking, we can say that they function to make a point that is then supported by a brief argument, purpose clause, explanation, or analogy. At times James even breaks into what could be called diatribe style, and even uses speech which is in character — for example, when he allows those Christians who practice discrimination in the Christian community (2:3), or those who refuse to help the needy (2:16), or those who have faith but no deeds (2:18), or those who boast of future plans (4:13) to speak briefly for themselves. This is not surprising in a piece of deliberative rhetoric such as we find in James.[31]

Not only do we have the imaginary interlocutor in the diatribe style in James; we also have the typical posing of direct, pithy questions which are instantly answered (3:13; 4:14; 5:13-14), as well

31. On the whole issue of rhetoric in the New Testament, see my little textbook, *New Testament Rhetoric.*

as the posing of numerous rhetorical questions to draw the audience into thinking like the author does. Often these occur in clusters, served up one right after the other for maximum effect (2:4-7, 14, 16, 20; 3:11-12; 4:1, 4-5). The voice of the author begins to emerge in such material, and it is clearly the voice of an authority figure who is pushing the audience to change their *behavior*. Sometimes he even becomes rather impatient with them. Thus we have short warnings or chiding remarks like "Don't be mistaken" (1:16) and "You know this" (1:19), and "Do you know?" and "Do you see?" (2:20, 22), and even the admonitory "This ought not to be so" (3:10) and the exasperated "Come now!" (4:13; 5:1).

Equally clear is that this hortatory discourse is one which was meant to be heard, drawing as it does on a full range of oral and aural rhetorical devices in Greek. For example, James readily uses rhythm and rhyme (see 3:6-7 on the former; see 1:6, 14; 2:12; 3:16; 4:8 for the latter), and he clearly has a strong penchant for alliteration, particularly the "p" sound (1:2-3, 11, 17, 22; 3:2), the "d" sound (1:1, 6, 21; 2:16; 3:8), and the "k" sound (2:3; 4:8), to mention but a few examples. Especially telling is the alliteration in 3:5: *mikros melos megala*. There is effective wordplay as well: *apeiratos/peirazei* (1:13) and *adiakritos/anupokritos* (3:17).

This is a document meant to be read aloud to good rhetorical effect — or, better said, it is meant to be delivered or performed in a rhetorically effective manner. Of the roughly 560 words in this discourse, 60 are not found elsewhere in the New Testament. Our author certainly isn't just repeating what he has heard before, or simply passing on early Christian tradition. He is a master of his source material, and when one notices how much of the document reflects these sorts of rhetorical devices in Greek, it becomes nearly impossible to imagine this homily being a translation from Aramaic rather than something composed originally in Greek.

Much has been made of the "catchword connection" in James, such that separate statements are linked on the basis of catchwords. This has sometimes led to the conclusion that these statements are linked only because they involve similar catchwords or phrases, or similar-sounding words. For example, Martin Dibelius noted this phenomenon and concluded that there is no "continuity of thought" in such material.[32] For the most part this conclusion is false when it comes to the book of James.

In the majority of cases there is a connection of sense as well as sound and key words in such linked materials, but the audience is sometimes expected to supply the missing premise in the enthymeme. There are a few cases where the connection seems to be merely a matter of wordplay (the connection of thought is not clear in 1:12-13, for example), but these sorts of examples are rare. In fact, while on the surface James appears beguilingly simple, this text expects a lot from its audience; they must participate in order to reach full understanding. For example, this text presupposes the audience's ability to pick up allusions to earlier sapiential material (some of it in the LXX, and some of it from Jesus' teaching), their ability to understand how such sapiential material functions in deliberative rhetoric as part of argumentation by exhortation, and their ability to make logical connections between remarks when one or another premise of an enthymeme is left out.

Our author is known for his vivid language, especially his vivid comparisons, using the rhetorical device of *synkrisis,* which is also found in such abundance in that other sermon we first examined in this chapter — Hebrews. Here, however, the comparison serves the purpose of urging the audience to change their behavior, and so, not surprisingly, our author isn't satisfied with comparing and contrasting what is good and what is "better." He uses analogies most frequently to show what behavior is bad or forbidden or even evil — whether the comparison is with a wave whipped up by the wind (1:6), foliage that withers in the sun (1:10-11), a raging fire in a forest (3:5-6), or fresh or brackish water (3:11).

32. Martin Dibelius, *A Commentary on the Epistle of James* (Philadelphia: Fortress Press, 1976), pp. 5-6.

But our author uses sapiential examples not only from nature but from human behavior as well: the taming of wild animals (3:7), the reining in of a horse (3:3), the steering of a ship (3:4).

Sometimes in his comparisons or implied comparisons James also draws on exemplary figures from hoary antiquity such as Job (see 2:21-25; 5:10-11, 17-18), but notice how differently they function than the examples cited in Hebrews 11. Sometimes the use of vivid language in James serves as a sort of rhetorical wake-up call to the audience, warning them about misbehavior, and sometimes it is clearly used for its shock value — for example, when our author speaks of the tongue being a world of wickedness. One needs to know how such sapiential language works to understand its intended effect. Sapiential rhetoric is often compressed into pithy or even paradoxical maxims with brief support in order to make them both memorable and memorizable. The implications require a certain unpacking, and the density of the ideas is deliberate, intended to force meditation and reflection. The analogies, of course, can't be taken literally, but the modern warnings about "not over-pressing figurative language" shouldn't diminish their bite. James is more than a clever wordsmith or pundit; he is an authoritative teacher who wants to effect behavioral change among the Jewish Christian communities in the Diaspora.

In the study of James that I did about fifteen years ago, I concluded that James was mostly conventional wisdom of a generic sort, perhaps written to an audience in Antioch in the form of a circular letter. I have since rethought and revised these conclusions. For one thing, the use of Jesus' sayings in this document is anything but a mere reiteration of conventional Jewish sapiential material. Rather, it reflects a combination of conventional and counter-order wisdom for a particular subset of the Christian community — Jewish Christians. As such, it is addressed to Jewish Christians throughout the Empire but outside of Israel, not just in Antioch or Asia Minor. Of course, there is traditional Jewish wisdom material here about the taming of the tongue, but it is juxtaposed with Jesus' own critique of wealth and the wealthy. And that is what makes this document so remarkable: like the teaching of Jesus, it offers something old and something new drawn from the resource of Jewish wisdom material. It will be instructive to set out a brief list of comparative texts from both the LXX and the Jesus tradition insofar as they have echoes in James:

Proverbs 3:34	James 4:6
Proverbs 10:30	James 3:18
Proverbs 10:12	James 5:20
Sirach 15:11-20	James 1:12-18[33]
Sirach 19:6-12; 20:4-7,17-19; 35:5-10; 38:13-26	James 3 in general

More extensive are the parallels with the Matthean form of the Q sayings of Jesus that we find in the Sermon on the Mount.[34]

Matthew 5:11-12/Luke 6:22-23	James 1:2
Matthew 5:48	James 1:4
Matthew 7:7	James 1:5
Matthew 7:11	James 1:17
Matthew 7:24/Luke 6:46-47	James 1:22
Matthew 7:26/Luke 6:49	James 1:23
Matthew 5:3, 5/Luke 6:20	James 2:5
Matthew 5:18-19 (cf. Luke 3:9)	James 2:10
Matthew 5:21-22	James 2:11
Matthew 5:7/Luke 6:36	James 2:13
Matthew 7:16-18/Luke 6:43-44	James 3:12
Matthew 5:9	James 3:18

33. On this, see D. Bertrand, "Le fond de l'epreuve: Epitre de Jacques 1:12-18," *Christus* 30 (1983): 212-18.

34. This has been laid out convincingly and discussed fully by P. J. Hartin, *James and the Q Sayings of Jesus* (Sheffield: Sheffield University Press, 1991), pp. 144-45.

Matthew 7:7-8	James 4:2-3
Matthew 6:24/Luke 16:13	James 4:4
Matthew 5:8	James 4:8
Matthew 5:4/Luke 6:25	James 4:9
Matthew 7:1-2/Luke 6:37-38	James 4:11
Matthew 6:19-21/Luke 12:33	James 5:2-3
Matthew 7:1/Luke 6:37	James 5:6
Matthew 5:11-12/Luke 6:23	James 5:10
Matthew 5:34-37	James 5:12

P. H. Davids was right to conclude on the basis of this evidence that "while James ultimately has wisdom material as his background, this is refracted . . . through the pre-gospel Jesus tradition."[35] The parallels above rule out the earlier suggestions that James was not originally a Christian document, or was not very Christian in character. To the contrary, as W. H. Wachob has recently argued in detail, James seems to have come out of the same or an allied community to that which produced the pre-Matthean Sermon on the Mount.[36] We notice several things when analyzing these parallels more closely. First of all, James rarely cites the sayings of Jesus directly. Rather, he weaves various ideas, themes, and phrases into his own discourse. He then presents this material as his own teaching, not the sayings of Jesus, though one may suspect that the audience would recognize the echoes. Also, it doesn't appear that Matthew is drawing on James or vice versa; rather, it appears that both are drawing on common source material. This in turn suggests, though it does not prove, that the Matthean form of the sayings of Jesus is closer to the original form than the Lukan form.[37]

35. P. H. Davids, "The Epistle of James in Modern Debate," *ANRW* 25, no. 5 (1988): 3622-684; here p. 3638.

36. See W. H. Wachob, *The Voice of Jesus in the Social Rhetoric of James* (Cambridge: Cambridge University Press, 2000).

37. On this, one can compare Witherington, *The Gospel of Matthew* (Macon, Ga.: Smyth & Helwys, 2006).

What do we learn about early Christian worship from James? Several very important things. The worship service is apparently open to invited guests — particularly, one would surmise, other fellow Jews. At the same time, James is concerned that the impartiality which characterizes God and characterized the ministry of Jesus should characterize conduct in the house church meetings, which he quite readily refers to as "synagogues," a Jewish word for assemblies. He is not at all pleased with favoritism in terms of seating order given to the rich over the poor, and notice that he expects there to be both sorts of persons in Christian worship. There are definitely leaders in these Christian meetings: James 5:14 refers to "the elders of the church," who are the ones who should be called upon to pray over and anoint the sick so they may get well. This is probably a direct carryover from one of the roles of elders in the non-Christian Jewish synagogues. The community meeting was also expected to be a place of transparency where believers would confess their sins. Notice that absolutely no reference is made to confessing to a priest or to a particular minister; believers are to confess to each other. James's pastoral concerns are evident throughout, right to the end of the sermon, where he talks about working for the restoration of someone who has wandered from the truth.

Like his brother, James is deeply concerned with the issue of the negative effects of wealth on the individual's spiritual life and, indeed, on the community's life, when others start fawning over and giving deferential treatment to the wealthy. This is a subject he addresses three times in this single sermon! He is, of course, very concerned as well with a faith that works, a living faith that leads to certain kinds of behavior and deeds of charity and piety. "Faith without works is dead" is perhaps the sermon's most famous line, but it could have been said by any Jewish proclaimer of that age, including Jesus or Paul. Finally, James is acutely aware of the dangers of the misuse of the tongue. In a small religious community, gossip, back-biting, innuendo, and the like are divisive and deadly, and James seeks to put a stop to them. This sermon is full of such practical wisdom, a wisdom James wanted to be delivered universally when Jewish Christians met throughout the Empire.

And this brings us to an important point. We are perhaps used to thinking of early Christian communities as being blends of Jews and Gentiles. After all, Galatians 3:28 intimates that this is the way things ought to be. The reality was quite otherwise. James, Peter, the Beloved Disciple, Jude, and the author of Hebrews were part of the division of labor directed toward Jews, the mission to Jews, and this in turn led to numerous, largely Jewish congregations (with perhaps some God-fearers) all over the Empire. This is whom James is addressing. By and large, the amalgamation of all Christians into unified congregations didn't happen at the beginning of Christian history. One of the clearest pieces of evidence of this being true as late as the late 50s A.D. is Paul's letter to the Romans, which turns out to be largely an exhortation to Roman Gentiles (see Rom. 11:13). There are Jewish Christians in Rome; they returned after the ban of Claudius lapsed in A.D. 54. But they're second-class citizens, and Paul wants them to be embraced by the Gentile Christians in Rome. They don't seem to have been worshipping together regularly. As it turns out, the division of labor agreed to, which is alluded to in Galatians 2:7-9, was a landmark determinant of things. Yes, Paul preached in synagogues wherever he went, but his main task was evangelizing Gentiles, and that's largely what he did. He began with Jews, but probably converted only a few of those, who in turn became some of his local house church leaders reaching out to Gentiles — people like Stephanus in Corinth or Lydia in Philippi. For every Titus who worked with Paul, there were two Timothys or Priscillas, but their focus was on Gentiles, and Paul's communities were largely Gentiles.

In fact, it was true that Peter and Paul and their co-workers traversed much of the same territory in their proselytizing, and the result was largely Jewish Christian congregations and largely Gentile Christian congregations and networks co-existing in the very same region or city. A good example of this can be found in Asia Minor and Galatia, where Paul certainly had house churches in Ephesus, Pisidian Antioch, Iconium, and Colossae. But in that same region John of Patmos addressed his congregations in Ephesus, Laodicea, and Colossae, and these do *not* seem to be the Pauline churches.

Paul Trebilco has helped us to see that the Johannine communities emanating from Ephesus and the Pauline ones would have recognized each other as Christians, and may well have cooperated at times, but in fact were two different groups of congregations.[38] This leads to a further point. It may well be the case that worship life in largely Jewish Christian congregations looked a little different than worship life in largely Gentile Christian congregations — for example, like the Pauline one in Corinth. In fact, it will be instructive for us to look at a cross-section of 1 Corinthians briefly before we conclude this chapter on early Christian worship. But let me stress here that the overall impression that one gets from a close look at sermons like Hebrews, 1 John, and James is that sermons in early Christianity were ethically serious and theologically challenging. They drew on previous traditions and sacred texts, but these were filtered through the Jesus tradition and through new Christological thinking. What we do not find in these sermons is generic, oversimplified, watered-down pablum served up to the masses. Perhaps this is the case in part because it was assumed that the audience had a relatively good grasp of the Old Testament and the Jewish tradition — which is more than we may be able to assume today about Christians and their tradition.

---

38. Paul Trebilco, *The Early Christians in Ephesus: From Paul to Ignatius* (Tübingen: Mohr, 2004), pp. 592-93; and see my discussion at length in Witherington, *Letters and Homilies for Hellenized Christians*, vol. 1 (Downers Grove, Ill.: InterVarsity Press, 2006), pp. 598-603.

Meals, Messages, and Ministers in Corinth

Without question, 1 Corinthians is a problem-solving letter. Actually, it is a deliberative discourse meant to be delivered orally in Corinth by a Timothy or a Titus to help sort out the many issues arising from that divided congregation. More specifically, 1 Corinthians is a discourse on concord, on overcoming those divisions.[39] Perhaps here more than anywhere else in the New Testament we get a glimpse into the interior life of an early Christian community. Unfortunately, what we discover when we open the door to that house church is a royal mess, which Paul is trying to clean up. It is thus only with extreme caution that 1 Corinthians can be used to tease out the nature of early Christian worship in homes, and even then, it may tell us more about the idiosyncrasies of this particular congregation in Corinth than about the nature of early Christian worship in general. Nothing in Hebrews, 1 John, or James really prepares us for what we hear about in 1 Corinthians: the chaos caused by a cacophony of Spirit-inspired voices of prophets, teachers, tongue speakers, and others, all vying for air time in the worship service. When my students occasionally say, "If only we could get back to first-century church life," my response typically is, "Which church would you like to serve — First Church Corinth, perhaps? Or how about First Church Laodicea?" My point is that church life then as now involves far-from-perfect human beings, and while there is much good to learn from the early church, we shouldn't rhapsodize about how ideal and perfect early Christian worship was.

Part of our difficulty in grasping what's going on in 1 Corinthians is that we don't understand the social setting of the material. Oddly enough, for example, 1 Corinthians has been taken to demonstrate that early Christians didn't believe in paying their

---

39. See Witherington, *Confict and Community in Corinth* (Grand Rapids: Wm. B. Eerdmans, 1994).

ministers because Paul chose to support himself by tent-making there. Never mind that in Philippians and 2 Corinthians 8–9 Paul admits that he received funds from the Philippians, which he was glad to have and use. Did the followers of Jesus believe that ministers deserved to earn their living by sharing the Gospel and doing pastoral and evangelistic work? To answer this question, and particularly the question of why Paul acted as he did in Corinth, we must back up and get a running start.

The basic principle, first enunciated by Jesus himself and then reiterated by Paul and others, is that "a workman is worthy of his hire" (Luke 10:7; cf. 1 Tim. 5:18). Let us start with Matthew 10:10 and parallels. Here Jesus is commissioning the twelve, the leaders in training among his followers, to go out two by two, and he quite specifically tells them not to take this or that money with them. Why? Because he expects them to rely on the system of standing hospitality and let others provide for them. This is why he says, "A workman is worthy of his hire/keep," and also why he tells them *not* to take any copper or gold or silver in a moneybag with them (v. 9). They should not expect to pay their own way. They are those commissioned to further the Kingdom, and they deserve to be paid for their work. So what is the source of the idea of "no-pay" ministers and faith-based missions where workers pay their own way? It comes from a rather bad misinterpretation of 1 Corinthians 9 and 2 Corinthians 11 — two texts we need to consider.

Social context is crucial to understanding these texts. One needs to know something about the patronage and clientage system operating in Corinth to understand why Paul chose Corinth in particular to offer the Gospel free of charge without receiving patronage or fees for speaking. The principle that Jesus first enunciated in Matthew 10:10 and Luke 10:7 is reiterated by Paul in 1 Corinthians 9:14-15: "The Lord has commanded that those who preach the Gospel should receive their living from the Gospel. But I have not used any of these rights."

In fact, throughout this passage Paul insists that he has a right to such support, a right to be paid, a right to be supported and taken care of. But *voluntarily* he has chosen not to take advantage of that right. Why? To answer this question, we need to understand that particular social situation and its difference from our own.

In first-century Corinth, there would have been orators, rhetoricians, sophists, and teachers for hire. Some were itinerant and would come to an agora (a gathering place), set out their moneybags, speak or sing for a time, and then ask for money. Others, more sophisticated, would engage in longer-term relationships with patrons. Paul didn't do the former for the very good reason that he wanted to do church planting and stay for a while. He wanted to establish relationships with those he was evangelizing.

He didn't want to appear to be a snake-oil salesman hawking some message he wasn't prepared to defend and explain over the long haul. On the other hand, he wanted to avoid the entangling alliances that were set up when one accepted patronage. So in Corinth he chose to support himself by tent-making, though he makes it perfectly clear in 1 Corinthians 9 that he had a right to be paid for his ministerial work if that's what he wanted. What is said in this chapter should be compared to what is said in 2 Corinthians 11:7-9. Notice that he calls it "lowering himself" or making a sacrifice when he chooses to preach in Corinth without a fee. But the next two verses are crucial: "I robbed other churches by receiving support from them so as to serve you. And when I was with you and needed something . . . the brothers and sisters from Macedonia supplied what I needed."

Now was there a difference between Paul's relationship with the Corinthian church and his relationship with the Philippian one? Yes — in every way. Paul had a relationship of "giving and receiving" with that church in Macedonia, as he says clearly in Philippians. He didn't have such a relationship with the Corinthian church. Why not? Because the Corinthian Christians were immature, and those who could have supported him wanted him to become their client on an ongoing basis. This would have obligated him in ways that would have limited his travel.

It is interesting that in Romans 16 Paul tells us about Phoebe from the church near Corinth in Cenchreae. She did become his *prostatis,* or supporter, at least for a time, but she must have understood that Paul was being remunerated in this way, not obligated to an ongoing future service to the patron. Clearly, we need to understand the technical language about funds and cultural practices in order to understand what Paul says about paid ministers.

There is also a further technical phrase we find in several places in the New Testament, including Romans and the Johannine Epistles: "sending me on my way" or "sending him on his way" (see 3 John 6 and Rom. 15:24). This refers to providing traveling money and supplies so that the preacher could get to the next destination. Paul says he was hoping the Roman church would provide this so that he could go on to Spain.

Let's look at one more important Pauline text — Galatians 6:6: "Those who receive instructions in the Word should share all good things with their instructor." This, of course, is a reference to a local congregational teacher, and the obligation of the congregation to provide for him. The English phrase "all good things" is really too general. What is meant here is providing monetary support *in addition to* room, board, and so forth. Indeed, Paul believed a workman to be worthy of his hire, just as Jesus said. In this context we can better understand some of the tensions between Paul and his Corinthians in regard to matters of worship.

The problem in a nutshell was this: While the Corinthians were highly spiritually gifted, too many of them were spiritually immature and egocentric in the bargain. Furthermore, they were only partially socialized into the Christian faith. Some of them were still attending banquets at pagan temples and scandalizing the Jewish Christians (a minority) who were in this congregation. The phrase "worship wars" is given new meaning by 1 Corinthians

8–10. Paul throws down the gauntlet and says, "You can't be partaking of the table of demons and the table of the Lord at one and the same time!" These Corinthians needed to choose which sort of worship they would be involved in.

We need to bear in mind that temples were in certain respects the most respectable ancient restaurants in the Greco-Roman world. There were dining rooms in temples where clubs, guilds, parties, politicos, and businessmen would meet regularly. This was where one made one's social contacts over a meal. To call such dining idolatrous and immoral would have seemed a bridge too far to some of Paul's new Gentile converts in Corinth. So what's an apostle to do?

Paul decides to order the Corinthians out of the pagan temples in 1 Corinthians 8–10, telling them what sort of worship they shouldn't be involved in. But then in 1 Corinthians 11–14 he corrects what's going on in the worship in house churches in Corinth. I want to emphasize this again: Paul is making a correction. We learn several things from this remarkable material. First of all, the Lord's Supper, at least in this setting, was taken in the context of a meal, and may well have been taken every time the Christians met together for worship.[40] Unfortunately, the usual stratification and pecking order of Greco-Roman meals had been imported into the Christian meal — with disastrous results. Some were coming late to the meeting — presumably the less well off, including slaves. And when they got there, not only had some gone ahead and gorged themselves and gotten inebriated — they hadn't left enough to share with others! This was hardly a meal characterized by *koinonia*, in contrast to what is described at the end of Acts 2. Christian worship in Corinth also involved praying, prophesying, exhorting, and speaking in tongues, among other activities, and presumably, since Greco-Roman protocols were involved, this would happen at the

---

40. See my lengthy discussion in *Making a Meal of It: Rethinking the Theology of the Lord's Supper* (Waco, Tex.: Baylor University Press, 2007).

symposion, the after-dinner speaker's conversation time at the drinking party, usually reserved for men. Paul, however, is fine with women praying and prophesying at appropriate times in worship, as long as they have their heads covered.[41]

This worship service might take place in a house, but strangers were allowed in, the so-called *idiotes* or uninitiated, and especially for this reason, Paul wanted more order and organization and less chaos in the prophesying and speaking-in-tongues portion of the worship service (1 Cor. 14:24). Apparently the Corinthian understandings of prophecy were about as Christian as their understanding of meals, which is to say that they had brought into the church their Greek notions about prophecy at the oracle of Delphi or at the Temple of Apollo in Corinth. In other words, they saw prophecy as something that was so ecstatic that one could not and should not try to control it. But Paul counters this, saying that one can wait and that believers can take turns prophesying. Furthermore, the Corinthians thought that it was appropriate to ask the prophet or prophetess leading questions for the sake of personal guidance. This is, of course, what happened at the oracles in antiquity: one went and asked practical questions like "Should I marry this person?" "Should I buy this land?" "Will I recover my health?" I would suggest that this is why Paul tells some of the wives not to interrupt the worship service with these sorts of questions, but to ask their husbands at home instead (1 Cor. 14:35). It would appear that prophets and also unauthorized teachers caused repeated problems in early Christian worship, and we see evidence of this not only in 1 Corinthians but also in Jude and in Revelation 2–3, and in 1 John and the Didache as well. In Mark 13 Jesus had warned that there would be false prophets and bad teachers in the eschatological age, and there were.

So how does Paul deal with this plethora of problems without quenching the Spirit and the spiritual gifts in Corinth, for which

41. On this, see pp. 22-25 above.

he is actually thankful (1 Cor. 1)? The answer is order, organization, and exhortation so that the body can function in harmony and with love and respect for its various members. Paul deconstructs the way they were conducting worship, including the way they were doing the meals, but it is clear from 1 Corinthians 14 that he is fine with genuine prophesying and teaching and speaking in tongues (with interpretation) within worship. The new wine did indeed *require* new wineskins, but what is interesting about the new wineskins is that to a large extent they were made in a shape very similar to that of the old wineskins. In early Christian practice there were still prayers, singing, almsgiving, preaching, and a Lord's Supper liturgy. There was still a need for leadership, for apostles, elders, and others. Charles Scobie is right: "The most remarkable discontinuity between OT and NT ministries is the total absence of the office of priest in the early Christian church."[42] However, this didn't mean that there wouldn't be both local and trans-local church leaders in the new order of things. But the subject of paid ministers does raise in an acute way the whole issue of the relationship of work and worship, especially for those whose work involves leading worship! In our next chapter we will consider this issue as part of our discussion of what eschatological worship really involves.

Questions for Reflection and Discussion

1. What role should preaching play in Christian worship?
2. Why was the proclamation of the living Word of God so crucial in an oral culture? Does the fact that we live in a text-based and more literate culture change the way we view preaching? Should it change our views?

42. Charles H. H. Scobie, *The Ways of Our God* (Grand Rapids: Wm. B. Eerdmans, 2003), p. 637.

3. What is rhetoric, and why was it important for Paul to use rhetoric in the proclamation of the Gospel, especially to Greco-Roman people?
4. Explain the three different senses in which the phrase "Word of God" is used in the New Testament. What is the common link between these three different uses?
5. Are there sermons in the New Testament outside the book of Acts? If so, give examples, and explain how this should affect the way we look at this or that biblical book.
6. How did the earliest Christians use the Old Testament in their preaching and teaching?
7. Should the Lord's Supper be shared in the context of a fellowship meal? What are the advantages and disadvantages of this practice? Do you think the New Testament mandates a particular way that the Lord's Supper should be shared?

CHAPTER SEVEN

Work and Worship: Labors of Love?

The Roots of Violence:
Wealth without work,
Pleasure without conscience,
Knowledge without character,
Commerce without morality,
Science without humanity,
Worship without sacrifice,
Politics without principles.

Mohandas K. Gandhi

Ora et Labora: Prayer and Work

What has impeded an adequate definition of worship? Both an understanding of the things it is related to in the Bible and an understanding of the things with which it is contrasted. Truly understanding worship entails, first, understanding what its antonym is: idolatry, which has an inherent connection with immorality (see Rom. 1:18-32), just as there is an inherent connection between true worship and morality, worship being the ultimate ethical act. Second, it entails understanding the relationship between work and worship. Until one defines work, one cannot know what worship

is, and vice versa. Notice the connection: the Fourth Commandment involves the cessation of work *on the day of worship* (Exod.
20:10 — "You shall not do any work"). The rabbis eventually for-
mulated thirty-nine distinct categories of work, each of which was
further subdivided (*M. Shabbat*, 7.2) — including sowing, plow-
ing, reaping, binding sheaves, threshing — and all of these were to
be avoided on the day of worship.[1]

But of course Exodus 20:10 is talking about Old Testament
worship, and it is a much-debated question whether one should
see New Testament worship as a further investment in a sabbatical
plan. In England, "everything stops for tea," but should it be true
for all Christians that "everything stops for worship"? Here we can
make a distinction between the act of worship and the day on
which worship happens. One can argue that, yes, worship should
be one's only focus when one is worshipping, but need that mean
that for the rest of the day one does nothing else? Has the coming
of Easter really not changed the situation at all in regard to work
and worship?

There are hints in the New Testament that the situation *has*
been altered by the inbreaking Kingdom in several respects. First
of all, there is the fact that the "day" of worship has changed, but
the definition of when the Sabbath occurs does *not* change.
Throughout the New Testament, both early and late, Sabbath
means the seventh day of the week from sundown Friday to sundown Saturday. Sunday is not called "the Sabbath" anywhere in
the New Testament; indeed, as we have already noted, it is regularly called "the first [day after] the Sabbath." The matter could
hardly be clearer. For Christians the axis of worship has shifted,
but not the day called Sabbath.

There are as well the rather remarkable statements of Paul
which we find in the New Testament. In Galatians 4:8-11 he tells

1. See L. R. Helyer, *The Witnesses of Jesus, Paul, and John* (Downers Grove,
Ill.: InterVarsity Press, 2008), p. 208.

his largely Gentile audience not to get caught up in special days, months, seasons, years — in short, not to follow the Jewish religious calendar. In Colossians 2:16-17 he urges a similar audience, "Therefore do not let anyone judge you by what you eat or drink, or with regard to a religious festival, a New Moon celebration or a Sabbath day. These are but the shadows of the things that were to come; the reality, however, is found in Christ." In that same document he warns against the worship of angels, whether this means actually giving adoration to angels or joining with angels in some sort of angelic visionary experience of heavenly worship. It is clear that Paul wants to distinguish Christian worship from his own Jewish heritage in various ways.[2] In light of the spiritual resurrection they have experienced, Paul exhorts his audience, "Set your hearts on things above, where Christ is seated at the right hand of God. Set your minds on things above, not on earthly things. For you died, and your life is now hidden with Christ in God. When Christ, who is your very life, appears, then you also will appear with him in glory" (Col. 3:1-4). This could almost be a description of what happens to John of Patmos in his visionary experience described in Revelation 5.

But to really understand how much this contrasts with other sorts of worship, we need to look at the passage just before Colossians 3, where Paul speaks in similar terms:

> Since you died with Christ to the elemental teachings of this world, why, as though you belong to this world, do you submit to its rules: "Do not handle! Do not taste! Do not touch!" These rules which have to do with things that are all destined to perish with use are based on merely human commands and teachings. Such regulations have the appearance of wisdom, with

2. For more discussion of these passages, see Witherington, *The Letters to Philemon, the Colossians, and the Ephesians* (Grand Rapids: Wm. B. Eerdmans, 2007).

their self-imposed worship, their false humility, and their harsh treatment of the body, but they lack any value in restraining sensual indulgence. (Col. 2:20-23)

There is much that is striking about this material, but for our purposes what is crucial is the contrast between the heavenly focus of Christian worship and these other worship patterns — and this includes the contrast with the abstentions involved in other forms of worship. Paul does not favor a pointless asceticism, not least because it may punish the body but not restrain "the flesh" — sinful human inclinations. In light of the previous verses in Colossians 2:16-17, it's hard to doubt that Paul is including in his warnings a return to old sabbatical patterns, which are seen as mere foreshadowings of the Christ and the Christ event. Put in our terms, Paul would be saying, "That's not Christian or Kingdom worship." Christian worship focuses on the exalted Christ and remembers that one already has the spiritual transformation, the spiritual reality, the dying and rising with Christ, of which these earlier regulations were only foreshadowings. Notice especially not only the exhortation to focus on the Christ who is in heaven now, but also the final reminder in Colossians 3:4 that Christ, who is the source and essence of the believer's new life, will be returning, and the Christian will appear with him in glory — possibly an allusion to the resurrection that believers will one day share with the risen Lord. The eschatological way of talking about worship, and what it does and doesn't entail, is very striking here. But there is more.

The fundamental reason why Christian worship should be different is not because Christ has inaugurated his kingdom on earth, but because believers are different and should worship differently. Notice how Colossians 1:13-14 puts it: "He has rescued us from the dominion of darkness and brought us into the Kingdom of the Son he loves, in whom we have redemption, the forgiveness of sins." Or consider Colossians 3:10-11: "[You] have put on the

We Have Seen His Glory

new self, which is being renewed in knowledge in the image of its Creator. Here there is no Greek or Jew, circumcised or uncircumcised, barbarian, Scythian, slave or free, but Christ is all, and is in all." Now I submit that Christian worship should be living out of the new realities, the new life we have in Christ, the new focus on the heavenly Christ who will one day return, and not focusing on anything earthly: the old earthly forms of worship, the old ascetical practices, the old ethnic, social, and sexual distinctions (on the latter, see Gal. 3:28).

Paul envisions a more universal form of worship which recognizes that the "eschatological already" is such that we are new creatures in Christ and should be praising God in a bolder, more upward, forward-looking way, dwelling no more in the past. Among the things left behind are the sabbatical practices of the past, which include the practices in regard to work, it would seem clear. This seems to be foreshadowed even in Jesus' ministry on the Sabbath.

Say what you want about Jesus' repeated healings on the Sabbath; they certainly violated somebody's theology of work on that day. John 9 and the story of the healing of the man born blind makes this apparent, and of course we could point to various other stories in the Synoptic Gospels. Judging from Mark 1:21-28, Jesus was healing on the Sabbath from the very inception of his ministry — in this case, performing an exorcism.

In Jesus' view, the Sabbath was made for human good in the first place, and now that the Kingdom was breaking in, what better day to give people relief from what bewitched, bothered, bewildered, or ailed them? On various of these occasions there was no emergency, and Jesus could have waited until sundown and Sunday to grant relief, but he didn't. Is this because Jesus had come to believe that all good things could and should be done if they were done to the glory of God, even on the day of worship? Paul certainly suggests as much when he says, "And whatever you do, whether in word or deed, do it all in the name of the Lord Jesus, giving thanks to God the Father through him" (Col. 3:17). All acts of work should be doxological, and thus should be acts of worship. Whatever can be done in good faith and to the glory of God can and should be done not only on the day of worship, but *as worship.*

Paul says more surprising things in Romans 14 which can advance this discussion. There we find a lengthy discourse on eating or not eating, and on observing one day as sacred or observing all days as sacred. Paul's point is several-fold. One should only do what one can do in good faith, whatever one's convictions about food or sacred days. And everything that one does should be done giving thanks unto the Lord and should be done unto God's glory. In short, all actions should be doxological. Paul even adds a remark which — given that he is a former Pharisee — is most shocking: "I am convinced, being fully persuaded in the Lord [presumably alluding to Jesus' own teaching], *that nothing is unclean in itself.*" No food, no clothing, no days. There is no more division between the sacred and the mundane or the sacred and the profane except in a moral sense. The only uncleanness is moral uncleanness: immorality. It is perhaps equally shocking that in regard to food or the observance of this or that day as sacred, Paul is content to say, "Let each be persuaded in his own mind" (14:5b). Why this profound change in viewpoint from a former Pharisee who was still an ethically rigorous person? Paul explains in 14:17: "For the Kingdom of God does not consist of eating and drinking, but rather of righteousness, peace, and joy in the Holy Spirit, because anyone who serves Christ in this way is pleasing to God."

And now we've gotten to the nub of things. We are supposed to be Kingdom people, behaving as though the Kingdom has already come in part, at least in regard to the transformation of the inner self, the human heart. Any service done in the honor and to the glory of Christ that involves righteousness, peace, and joy is pleasing to God and is doxological — is a form of worship. Not perhaps worship and fellowship of the gathered community —

which we must not neglect, as the author of Hebrews reminds us (Heb. 10:25) — but nonetheless worship. All things that believers do in the Kingdom age should be doxological.

Sometimes someone asks me if I have a "quiet time," by which the inquirer means a time of devotion, and perhaps private study of God's Word, apart from other things. My response is that I'm trying to do all things unto the glory of God, and so whether I'm preparing a lecture, or developing a sermon, or writing a book, I try to do it in a doxological mode. The great partition between the sacred and the mundane has been torn down in Christ, just as the walls between races and genders and classes have been torn down. Furthermore, worship should be all about love, joy, peace, and righteousness, and it should reflect the rainbow coalition of peoples that are in Christ.

In this part of the discussion I've been skirting around the edges of the issue of work, and certainly the implications here are that worship on the Lord's Day doesn't require ceasing from all work on that day. But we need a better theological understanding of work, especially in light of the new eschatological truths we've been discussing.

Labora et Ora: Work and Prayer

One of the more notable differences between Old Testament and New Testament worship is how one may come to that worship. In Psalm 24:3-4, we read that in order to come into the presence of God, one must have both clean hands and a pure heart; no distinction is made between ritual and moral or outward and inward purity. In Christian worship, you may come as you are, but you should come with the expectation that you will not stay as you are, that you will be cleansed and transformed if you get caught up in the presence of God as a sanctifying force, get caught up in wonder, love, and praise. Christ's death and resurrection have made it possible for even sinners to draw nigh to their God without immediate negative repercussions. The church is not a museum for saints; it is a hospital for sinners where people come to get well. But what of those people for whom work is either their god or the bane of their existence, who have a false theology of work? If they have a false view of work, can they have a true view of worship? It is very unlikely. What is more likely is that they will view worship as just more hard or even boring work, a context in which one pays one's dues and gives respect to the ultimate taskmaster and slave driver: God.

Let's ask the question again: Why no Sabbath day in the New Testament? It's not because now it's all work and no play; it's because in the eschatological situation everything is supposed to be worship, whether or not it involves work. It's all supposed to be doxological. But can work be worshipful, a doxological act? Let's go back to square one in Genesis and see.

Unfortunately, work has gotten a lot of bad press due to a misreading of the curse God placed on Adam and Eve. Let's rewind the discussion to Genesis 1:28, before the Fall. This is what we hear: "And God blessed them and said to them 'Be fruitful and increase in number; fill the earth and subdue it. Rule over the fish in the sea and the birds in the sky and over every living creature that moves on the ground.'" God adds that Adam and Eve can eat whatever plants and fruits they want, as can the other creatures, and this statement is followed by this declaration: "God saw all he had made and done, and it was very good."

Now, multiplying and subduing the earth involve labor. Clearly there was work to be done *before* the Fall. Human beings created in God's image were expected to act as mini-creators and mini-rulers over the earth, reflecting God as the Great Creator and the Great Ruler. This was no small task. What the Fall brought into the picture was pain added to the labor. Both sorts of work — production and reproduction, farming and fertilizing (whether human or otherwise) — were going to involve labor pains.

Adam's curse was a curse on the ground, which was going to become less pliable, less responsive, bearing thorns and thistles among the plants of sustenance. Thus "by the sweat of your brow you will eat your food" (Gen. 3:19). As for Eve, she would experience pain in her childbearing, and she would be ruled by her husband: "to love and to cherish" would become "to desire and to dominate" (Gen. 3:16). It couldn't be a good thing for the mother of all that her main claim to fame was going to involve peril and pain. It is interesting that Paul in 1 Timothy 2:15 seems to argue that this curse is reversed through Mary, through the "childbearing" — namely, through the coming of the Messiah. However, the verse might just be a promise to faithful Christian women of the reversal of the curse. I myself prefer the former reading.

Thus, in sum, human beings were always intended to work, to fulfill the creation mandate, and God said that humans doing so was very good. Work per se is not the problem. It is the toilsomeness of work, the bone-wearying nature of it, the peril of it, the pain of it that is the problem. How, then, does the coming of the Kingdom change all this?

To begin with, the mandate changes. Notice that Jesus tells his disciples that they are free to not marry and propagate the species (Matt. 19:9-12), but can remain eunuchs (like him) for the sake of the Kingdom. Notice, too, that Paul says the same thing in 1 Corinthians 7, even insisting that marriage is a calling and that singleness is a calling — as he puts it, a "charisma," a gift of God's grace. Jesus simply says that each of these callings — fidelity in marriage and celibacy in singleness — are "for those to whom it is given." In the new creation, apparently, the original creation orders from headquarters are seen as fulfilled or eclipsed.

And then there is this: human beings are no longer called upon to rule the earth for God. Now that the Dominion has broken in, God, in the person of the God-man, has taken on that task. The last Adam is doing what the first Adam failed to do. Listen to

Colossians 2:9-10: "For in Christ all the fullness of the deity lives in bodily form, and in Christ you have been brought to fullness. *He is the head over every power and authority*" (emphasis mine). Now this remarkable statement makes clear that Christ, our representative, is ruling over all things, and that in him we, and presumably our creation-order tasks, have been fulfilled, filled out, completed. What does that leave for us to do?

The answer is still "ora and labora" (prayer and work), worship and work — only now not only worship but also work has been transformed and infused with new purpose and life. Now all work can be done to the glory of God without paying homage to the Fall or worrying about the wearying nature of it. If we have the gift of everlasting life, we don't have to worry about being worn out by work. Death has no dominion over us or our work. It is all fruitful in the Lord if good, and done unto the Lord.

We haven't been given a "work release" because we're saved — far from it. Paul tells us that we have been created in Christ Jesus for a whole new kind of work: for good works, works of piety and charity. "For we are God's handiwork, created in Christ Jesus for good works, which God prepared in advance for us to do" (Eph. 2:10). God already has our work orders drawn up in advance, in order to advance the Kingdom upon earth.

Now, all proper work is Christian service, and all is doxological. Any good thing worth doing is not only worth doing well — it's worth doing to the glory of God. This makes both logical and doxological sense. God is a doer, and we have been recreated in Christ to be doers as well.

Sometimes, of course, this can be pushed too far. This happens when we so identify who we are with what we do that we let our tasks define our beings and identities — we call ourselves by our tasks: doctors, lawyers, ministers. But this is simply "overdoing" it. The opposite of this is not doing nothing but doing things to God's glory, realizing that our identity comes from our new selfhood in Christ, not primarily from what we do. Doing doesn't define being; new being in Christ shows the parameters, the character, the nature, and the necessity of what we should do.

The Gospel is not Good News for slackers, or the indolent, or the lazy. Grace is not a pillow on which the slothful may rest; rather, it is an Energizer battery to charge and recharge us to do good works unto the glory of God. Did we really think that God would require less of us under grace than he did under Law, or less in the new creation than he did in the old one? No — "to whom more is given, more is required."

Paul has some stern words for those who refuse to work. And it will be helpful for us to consider them briefly before we close this chapter.

Let Those Who Will Not Work . . .

In one of his earliest letters, Paul tells the Thessalonians two things: not only must they support "those who work hard among you," referring to their ministers (1 Thess. 5:12), but they must also "warn those who are idle and disruptive" (1 Thess. 5:14). What Paul is referring to in his latter comment is the system of patronage that existed in the Greco-Roman world, where one sought to become a sycophant of some wealthy person, and one would do whatever he asked, but otherwise one would stand around and do nothing — waiting to be told what to do. Paul explains the matter further in 2 Thessalonians 3:6-13:

> In the name of the Lord Jesus Christ, we command you, brothers, to keep away from every brother who is idle and does not live according to the tradition you received from us. For you yourselves know how you ought to follow our example. We were not idle when we were with you, nor did we eat anyone's food without paying for it. On the contrary, we worked night and day, laboring and toiling so that we would not be a burden

to any of you. We did this not because we do not have the right to such help, but in order to make ourselves a model for you to follow. For even when we were with you, we gave you this rule: "If a man will not work, he shall not eat."

We hear that some among you are idle. They are not busy; they are busybodies. Such people we command and urge in the Lord Jesus Christ to settle down and earn the bread they eat. And as for you, brothers, never tire of doing what is right.

We are to be busy without becoming busybodies — nosing our way into other people's affairs. And the clarion imperative "Let the one who will not work, not eat" ought to settle once and for all that Christians are expected to work and earn their own living. But what about bearing one another's burdens? What about sharing? What about "all things in common," and no exclusive right to property? Paul certainly believed in sacrificial service and giving to others in need. He also believed in burden-sharing as well as burden-bearing. We can see his perspective on this in Galatians 6.

In Galatians 6:2, Paul says, "Carry each other's burdens, and so fulfill the Law of Christ," but then he turns around in Galatians 6:5-6 and says, "Each of you should carry his own load. Nevertheless, those who receive instruction in the word should share all good things with their instructor." What's going on in these verses? Has Paul contradicted himself? As it turns out, the answer is no. Paul uses one word for "burden" or "load" in the former verse, another word for it in the latter verses. This text is referring to exactly what Paul says in the passage from 2 Thessalonians 3 quoted above. People should not be sponging off others; they should make their own living if they are able to do so. Paul also says in these verses what he says elsewhere — namely, that a minister is a workman worthy of his hire (1 Cor. 9) and should expect the congregation to pay him for his work. This frees him up to focus on the ministerial work full-time. But what is Galatians 6:2 all about?

As it turns out, here Paul is referring to a specific command of Christ to be burden-sharers with one another, especially in the case of those who are in need (see Matt. 5:42). The word used here seems to refer to financial burdens in particular, and we see the sort of sharing alluded to here in Acts 2:43-47. There is a time and a place for burden-sharing, and there is a time and a place for carrying one's own load when one is able to do so. Thus, the apostle sets up a delicate balance between communal support for one another and individual responsibility when it comes to work. Paul affirms both here — and we might add that he set a clear example of what hard work, and not being a burden to others, looked like. We are reminded of Romans 13:8: "Owe no one anything except the debt of loving one another."

In his final meeting with the Ephesian elders, Paul reminds his audience of the lifestyle he chose to live while among them, setting an example: "I have not coveted anyone's silver or gold or clothing. You yourselves know that these hands of mine have supplied my own needs and the needs of my companions. In everything I did, I showed you that by this kind of hard work we must help the weak, remembering the words of the Lord Jesus: 'It is more blessed to give than to receive'" (Acts 20:33-35). Paul was no stranger to hard work (see, e.g., 2 Cor. 11 — the entire chapter), and he called others to imitate him. It is interesting that a person who believed he was no longer obligated to keep the Law or do "the works of the Mosaic law" nonetheless was equally convinced that the Law and the teachings of Jesus call us all to a higher level of striving and hard work.

Work can be a part of our worship, an element in our doxology, an expression of our faith, a measure of our devotion, a repaying of the debt of love. All that we say and do should be done unto God's glory, but corporate worship is the epicenter of that work of glorification. In our final chapter we must draw the threads of this study together and ask some careful questions about what worship in the shadow of the Kingdom should look like and could look like and would look like — if we might just catch the vision.

Questions for Reflection and Discussion

1. What are the differences between Old Testament and New Testament worship patterns, and what explains these differences? Why is it that Christians can't simply repeat Old Testament worship practices?

2. How did the coming of Jesus and the Kingdom he brought in change the nature and practice of worship?

3. One of the points emphasized in this chapter is that in Christian worship, you may come as you are, but you will not stay as you are — you will be cleansed and transformed if you get caught up in the presence of God as a sanctifying force. Discuss this idea. Why do you think that the New Testament writers don't insist on Christians observing a Sabbath?

4. What is the proper relationship between work and worship? In what sense should work be doxological? If work can't be done to the glory of God, should Christians do it?

CHAPTER EIGHT

Doxology: The End and Aim of All Things

A person will worship something, have no doubt about that. We may think our tribute is paid in secret in the dark recesses of our hearts, but it will out. That which dominates our imaginations and our thoughts will determine our lives, and our character. Therefore, it behooves us to be careful what we worship, for what we are worshipping we are becoming.

Ralph Waldo Emerson

Worship is many different things to many different people, and people's expectations about worship differ. Some are looking for a reliable, trustworthy link with their past — the worship of their mothers and fathers and grandparents, which conveys a sense of stability to them and their otherwise hurried and harried lives. Some are looking for energy, ecstasy, and joy in the morning, and they gravitate toward a more buoyant, less traditional service, perhaps one with high-energy music or the dramatic sharing of charismatic gifts. Some want a worship service that has a bit of mystery and liturgy to it; indeed, we are increasingly told that this is what postmoderns like. Some want pageantry and pomp and processions, smells and bells.

Some go to worship to be forgiven; some go just to forget.

Some go to visit with friends and see familiar faces. Some go because "duty calls" and they have to usher or be the lector for that Sunday. Some go because they feel a deep need to receive communion or the Eucharist. Some go because they want to pray with God's people for help and healing. Some even go for the coffee and doughnuts. There are many reasons why people go to church, and even more why they attend worship, but whatever their reasons for coming, too few of them really understand what worship is meant to be about. And as the biblical understanding ebbs and the consumer mentality flows and grows, it is hardly surprising that worship has been turned into something it was never intended to be: a performance of the few for the couch potatoes for Jesus in the pews. Let me relate two actual worship experiences, and you'll see why we need, in terms of orientation and understanding, an extreme makeover of our views on worship.

Tallulah Bankhead was a remarkable woman and big in her heyday in Hollywood. She talked loudly and dressed loudly; she hardly had a subtle bone in her body. She also wasn't much of a church-going gal, but she loved pomp and ceremony. When she heard that an archbishop was coming to New York and that there would be a major service with all the bells and whistles in his honor, she decided to go. (Already we have a problem here. Worship services are not to be performed for the honor and glory of some human being. Even funerals are not supposed to be that sort of service.) On that momentous day, Tallulah got all dressed up in her best chartreuse taffeta outfit, which included a giant bonnet, and off she marched to church. She got there early, before the eleven A.M. starting time, because she knew that while many are called, pews are chosen. She wanted to be right on the aisle so she could watch the procession as it came down the aisle toward the altar.

Sure enough, right at eleven A.M. things began to happen. After an improvised organ piece, the back doors of the cathedral opened, and the human stream began: the acolytes, followed by someone carrying a large cross, followed by someone carrying the

Bible, followed by the children's choir, followed by the adult choir, followed by the ordinary oblates, followed by the regular priests, followed by the local monsignor, followed by the bishop of the diocese. Finally, at the end of the procession came the archbishop, wearing a gold lamé robe and swinging a censor back and forth (so pretty soon the whole congregation was incensed). Tallulah was mesmerized by all this pageantry, and she couldn't take her eyes off the archbishop's robe. Instinctively, as he was about to pass her pew, she reached out and tugged on his sleeve and said in her famous gravelly voice, "Darling, your gown is divine, but your purse is on fire!"

Tallulah was definitely trying to enter into the moment, but she wasn't quite cognizant of what was going on. Like so many, she was on the periphery or penumbra of the act of worship and didn't really know how to participate properly. She was amazed, like the crowds in the synagogue were when Jesus healed someone, but she wasn't caught up in wonder and love and praise of God — instead, she was focused on the apparel of the archbishop. Amazement at the "shock and awe" of worship is not the same as adoration.

Let me relate one other worship experience at the other end of the scale. In a mega-church near Chicago (the name of which shall be left unmentioned), some in their wisdom decided that it was time to do "casual" worship in the extreme. The worship planners were deliberately and desperately trying to make their worship service more inviting and less intimidating to "seekers." The service went along much as it always did, and then in the middle there was a break in the music and an indication that something else was going to happen.

This got the attention of one "seeker." In fact, she came up to the senior minister after the service and said, "You know what I really liked about that service?" "No," the minister answered. "I liked it that, in the middle, we stopped and had snacks," she told him. What she was referring to was the break in the middle of the service when the Lord's Supper had been served, using Kool-Aid and cheese crackers! Reflecting on this encounter, the minister said later, "An unacceptable image arose in my mind during this conversation: 'This is my snack, given for you.'" Whatever else it is, the body and blood of Jesus Christ should never be confused with a snack! Here we see the extreme trivialization of the sacred.

So we have two examples. In the first, the service conveyed the sense of the sacred through ceremony, but perhaps focused too much on the archbishop and too little on God. In the second, the service abandoned the sense of the sacred for contact with the mundane and so ended up not conveying anything particularly holy to anyone. Indeed, some would say that sacrilege happened that day in that church.

How do we get back to having a clear and helpful understanding of worship, and, equally important, how do we get back to having an understanding based on the knowledge that we no longer dwell in the past? We are a people who once dwelt in darkness, but now we have seen a great light: the glory of God in the face of Jesus Christ. How do we get to a place where we understand our eschatological position between the now and the not yet, between the resurrection of Jesus and our own resurrection, and where we begin to look forward with unveiled faces?

At this point it will be helpful to review some of the things we've said along the way about true Christian worship:

Worship is recognizing who is the Creator and who is not.
Worship is recognizing who is the Redeemer and who is not.
Worship is union and communion.
Worship is not fellowship.
Worship is theocentric, not anthropocentric.
Worship is giving glory to God, and so becoming transfixed and transfigured.
Worshippers are not an audience; God is the audience of worship.

Worship is about adoration, celebration, and jubilation. Worship, while it celebrates the past mighty acts of God, should not seek to dwell in the past or make it the main focus. Worship is an act of love and hope and faith, and only secondarily an act of remembering.

New Testament worship doesn't look like Old Testament worship. It doesn't involve priests, temples, or sacrifices in the Old Testament sense of those terms. We are the temples in which God dwells. We are all, male and female, the priesthood of all believers, with Christ as our heavenly high priest. There is no intermediate or intermediary priesthood of the few between the worshipper and God in New Testament worship. And the only sacrifices involved are the sacrifice of self, of praise, and of service, not the re-sacrifice of Christ.

In Christian worship, only God's glory, not human glory, should be unveiled. God should be glorified; humans should be edified. This process is interesting because when humans encounter God in Christ, they also are transformed into a more glorious condition; they move along toward their destiny, which is to be fully conformed to the image of Christ. But that is God's act of sharing his glory and the glory of his Son with us. It is never a matter of human self-glorification, any more than God's basic character is self-centered.

In our review of the elements of earliest Christian worship, I noted the carryovers from synagogue worship: prayer, praise, and indeed various sorts of singing, reading of Scripture, preaching, and almsgiving, all done in a doxological mode — with reverence, with a sense of the holy, a sense of the sacred, with adoration, with joy, with exuberance, as an act of love fulfilling the First Commandment. I noted the worship scenes in heaven as described in places like Isaiah 6 and Revelation 4–5 and suggested that we were supposed to be living into those sorts of worship experiences. Indeed, here I would add that earthly worship is supposed to be sharing in the heavenly worship. Here I must mention the communion of saints.

The idea of the communion of saints is that there is only one people of God, whether on earth or in heaven, and since both groups are very much alive (indeed, the dead are paradoxically more alive than we earthlings, because they are right in the very presence of Life itself), we all *together* are and should be sharing in worship, fully aware of our eschatological situation. John's vision of worship inspired him to share in the act of worship, and I suggested that if we could catch a glimpse of such true worship, it would be life-transforming, as it would mean that we have caught a glimpse of our God.

The Bible says that without vision the people perish, and this is especially true without a vision of proper worship, for *worship is the means God uses to mold us into our better selves.* Worship is where we more nearly become our best selves, and become more like what we admire — namely, Jesus Christ, who, as Hebrews says, always lives to intercede for us as our heavenly High Priest right in the very presence of God.

Too often we go to worship and come away disappointed because the sermon was weak, the choir wasn't in tune, the congregation participated halfheartedly, and so on. But what if we went to worship because we had something to give rather than something to get? What if we realized that we are the ones who are not in tune with God, that we need a tune-up? John Donne, my favorite metaphysical poet, had something to say on this very subject:

> Since I am coming to that holy room,
>> Where, with thy choir of saints for evermore,
> I shall be made thy music; as I come
>> I tune the instrument here at the door,
>> And what I must do then, think here before.
>>>> "Hymn to God, My God,
>>>> in My Sickness," stanza one

Suppose we saw worship as not merely our audition for the heavenly choir but our chance to sing with the heavenly choir, who are off-camera, so to speak? Suppose we saw worship as our chance to tune our instruments and learn to praise God in a bolder way? Suppose it isn't necessary or inevitable that worship be the worst ship sailing on a Sunday morning? Suppose it could be something glorious that leads us into the very presence of our God, who leads us forward to the New Jerusalem, the final victory?

I don't think it's an accident that the last battle in the Bible is portrayed as part of the worship wars: the last battle is between the worshippers of the beast and the worshippers of the Christ. F. A. Murphy puts it this way: "The 'last battle' is not between good and evil as abstractly conceived but between the worshippers of the beast and the worshippers of God. The leitmotif of the Apocalypse is worship combined with judgment. The one who is worshipped is not simply a conquering hero, a symbol of power, but 'a Lamb standing, as though it had been slain' (5:6)."[1] Exactly. The ultimate issue in human history is this: *Who shall humans worship?* They waver between true worship and its moral ethos on one end of the spectrum, and idolatry and immorality on the other end, and it has ever been thus.

Why is this the ultimate issue in life, the ultimate issue in human history? Because human beings were created for worship, of course. It is that which is the aim and purpose of human beings at the end of the day: to recognize and celebrate their creaturehood by recognizing that only God is God, and they are not. Humans are not the masters of their own fate, not the captains of their own souls. They have been created in the image of God for *worship,* and all that that word entails. Worship is where the creation is finally in order, under and bowing down to the one true God of the universe. Humans have been created as "homo religiosus" — as

---

1. F. A. Murphy, "Revelation," in *Theological Interpretation of the New Testament,* ed. Kevin Vanhoozer (Grand Rapids: Baker, 2005), p. 246.

religious beings. As the Scottish saint John Knox put it, "The chief end or aim of humankind is to know God and to love and adore him forever." That is right. Worship is where we get caught up in that wonder and love and praise of God. Salvation is but a means to that end, a means of restoring us to a right relationship with God so that we can return to praising our Maker while we have breath.

As a Methodist, I find one of the most moving stories from our Methodist heritage to be that of the death of John Wesley in the tiny room next to City Road Chapel in London. John Wesley's last words were carefully recorded by those Methodists who had gathered near him at the end of his long and remarkable life. There were two things he kept saying: "Best of all, God is with us," and a line not from one of his brother's hymns but from Isaac Watts — "I'll praise my Maker while I have breath." There could be no better way to go on to Glory than by tuning up for the heavenly choir in this fashion. But Wesley knew well that God is already with us. We already encounter God here and now, and this is what surely should inspire and transform our worship.

What about charismatic worship? I must tell you that I love robust, enthusiastic worship — especially a good African-American service where everyone is caught up in the praise and presence of the Lord and worshippers are even dancing in the pews and aisles. I also love a good charismatic service where the result is the same even if the expressions vary. I think there is a reason why Paul says glossolalia is the tongues of angels (1 Cor. 13:1), and he is happy to speak in them frequently. He sees this as the language of heaven and heavenly worship, not merely a heavenly prayer language. We would have to ask whether prayers are being offered in heaven or only answered there, but that is a discussion for another day. Here I would suggest that charismatic worship at its best — without self-centered displays and chaos, and with the careful ordering that Paul says in 1 Corinthians 14 needs to be in place — is indeed a crossing of the line, or at least a blurring of the line, between earthly and heavenly worship.

Unfortunately, too often people evaluate worship and which sort they want to participate in on the basis of style, and this is a serious mistake. Worship should never be evaluated on the basis of mere style. (I can see a teenager on the old *American Bandstand* show saying, "This song has a bit of a beat, but I can't dance to it, so I can only give it a 7.5.") The issue is not style but *substance*. The issue is also not "where am I most comfortable." Did it never occur to you that worship might be most helpful when it unsettles your ways and makes you profoundly uncomfortable with your present state of spiritual lethargy?

I remember going to a worship service in the 1970s at Tremont Temple Baptist in downtown Boston. It was a Derek Prince healing and exorcism service. Being a good old Southern Methodist of high-church leanings, I had never seen anything like this before. There were people falling out into the aisles and screaming for exorcism; there were legs being healed or lengthened at the altar; there were people having hands laid on them so that they could receive the gift of tongues. Whatever else one could say about such a service, one could scarcely call it dull. In fact, it was frightening and electrifying to watch people come unglued in public. I was reminded of that very first synagogue service in Capernaum where Jesus exorcised an evil spirit (Mark 1:21-28). I'll bet that woke up the neighborhood too! After that service, I came to the conclusion that along with some pretending and counterfeiting and "wanna-be" behavior, some genuine spiritual transformations were also going on there.

I was reminded of some of the same sorts of experiences described as part of the revivals and camp meetings in the early nineteenth century in Kentucky and elsewhere. I suppose God does these things from time to time to wake us up to the truth that there is a spiritual battle going on in this life between good and evil, and, as F. A. Murphy says in the quote cited above, in the end the final human battle is a worship battle between idolatry and true worship. I also concluded that the Tremont service was a special healing occasion in worship, which is not, in the main, the focus of worship from week to week, not least because it would draw too much attention to the miracle and the healed rather than focusing on the Miracle Maker: Jesus. Some people go to such services for the same reason they stop to see what's happened in a car accident — pure morbid curiosity. And, unfortunately, too large a dose of "faith-healing" services leads to charlatan-like behavior and to the cult of human personality focusing on "the Human Healer." Why is it that we so often focus on the gift or the conveyer of the gift, rather than the Giver?

God must be laughing when preachers say, "I saved seventeen souls at that revival last week!" That declaration is rather like Shakespeare's pen announcing, "I wrote three wonderful plays last week!" No, it is God who saves, and God in Christ who heals, and more often than not what the minister needs to do is just open up wide and get out of the way of what God wants to do through her or him. Worship is not supposed to become a dog-and-pony show, or an exhibition of human exhibitionism, or in general an anthropocentric venture. The focus must be on God, and the glory must be given to God.

IN THE PREVIOUS CHAPTER we spent some time reflecting on the relationship between work and worship, and we concluded that one of the major differences between Christian worship and Old Testament worship is that we are the Easter people who celebrate on the day after the Sabbath, and we are not called to see worship as Sabbath or Sunday as Sabbath. Indeed, instead of separating the sacred from the mundane, we are called upon to *make all things sacred*, to let all things be doxological, done to the glory of God. We are called to make our worship doxological, done as an act of praise to God. But, as we noted, work is only part of doxology, only part of our worship. We are not to make the mistake of forsaking corporate worship, forsaking the joining of ourselves together, for God has promised to be especially present, Immanuel, wherever two or more are gathered.

I have sometimes heard this testimony: "I can worship God just as well out on the holy links and in the woods as in church." When this is not just an excuse to worship at Bedside Baptist, or Posturepedic Presbyterian, or St. Mattress Methodist, or Ever-Rest Episcopalian, there is in fact some truth to this, but not enough. You can certainly glorify the God of Creation by celebrating his presence through exploring and appreciating his creation. We see this very thing in the beautiful Psalm 8. The problem with doing that in lieu of going to church is that while you can encounter the work of God and general revelation in nature, you will not encounter the Word of God there, and the proclamation of his saving acts, and that is, of course, crucial. Worship involves the proclamation of the saving love of God week by week, and rightly so, because the least, the last, and the lost need to hear it and become the most, the first, and the found. At the end of the day, worship without a steady dose of special revelation and salvation is not adequate Christian worship. That is to say, worship without good preaching is not adequate worship, because God wants to clear his throat each week and address his people.

Christian worship should most often have a Christocentric focus. We saw how the earliest Christians made sure this was so in their writing of the new Christological hymns in praise and adoration of our Savior. And of course Christians today are still doing that. (I think of the praise song "In Christ Alone" by Keith Getty and Stuart Townend.) But there is something else that should characterize our worship: not merely self-forgetfulness instead of self-consciousness, but also a sense of detachment from worldly things and a sense of attachment to God in light of the new eschatological situation.

Paul describes this a bit in 1 Corinthians 7:29-31: "What I mean, brothers and sisters, is that the time has been shortened.

From now on, those who are married should live as if not, those who mourn as if not, those who are happy as if not, those who buy something as if it were not theirs to keep, those who use things of the world as if not engrossed in them. For the form of this world is passing away." Paul is calling for a strong sense of detachment from all worldly institutions, affairs, and things. He says that the form of this world, even including marriage (which is an institution inaugurated for our earthly good, not an eternal institution), is already passing away. Why is this so? Because the time has been shortened. (The Greek here says not "short" but "shortened.") What has shortened it? Obviously it is the Christ event, the death and resurrection of Jesus, and this means that the eschatological clock is ticking. Henceforth, we should tread lightly and be only lightly attached to the things of this world, for they will all pass away. We should remember this old Christmas hymn: "Let all mortal flesh keep silence, and with fear and trembling stand; ponder nothing earthly-minded, for with blessing in his hand, Christ our God to earth descendeth, our full homage [and worship] to demand." Just so, worship cannot go forward as usual in light of the Incarnation, death, and resurrection of Jesus.

It's not, however, simply a matter of detachment from the old; it's also a matter of attachment to the new, to the Christ. Remember the words of Paul in Colossians which we considered earlier in this study: "Set your heart on things above. . . . Set your mind on things above, not on earthly things" (Col. 3:1-2). Why? It's not just because Christ came and died and rose; it is because "you died, and your life is now hidden with Christ in God" (Col. 3:3). Christian worship must reflect the new spiritual realities, for the believer now lives between new birth and new body, just as we live between the Kingdom already come and the Kingdom yet to come.

The sense of detachment from earthly things should also lead to a sense of detachment from earthly anxieties; hence the further exhortation "Let the peace of Christ rule in your hearts. . . . Let the message of Christ dwell among you richly as you teach and admonish one another with all wisdom through psalms, hymns, and songs from the Spirit" (Col. 3:15-16). All is to be doxology, all done to the honor of Christ and the glory of God, and if the peace does indeed rule within the believer, then there is no cause or room for being overwhelmed by earthly anxieties and cares. Of course, there is a difference between leading a carefree existence and a careless one, which shows you could care less. We are the temples where God dwells; we are the body of Christ, where Christ dwells on earth; we are filled with the Spirit, and the Spirit has taken up residence in our realm. Worship can and must be different if these things be true, for our focus on God without is impelled and inspired and empowered by God within us and within the community. Christ in us is the hope of glory, and Christian worship should always have one eye on the prize, one eye on the eschatological finish line, where we will know as we are known and where we will all be changed into the perfect likeness of the Son.

We have studied at some length early Christian preaching, and it would be wise to emphasize here the importance of Scripture reading and preaching in worship, for it is when God addresses us! The rest of worship is directed from us to God. The reading of the Word and its proclamation moves in the opposite direction. What should truly meaningful preaching be like?

If it is like early Christian worship, it will be preaching that emphasizes the new life in Christ and the importance of Christocentric life and worship. This doesn't mean focusing just on Christ as savior, but also on Christ as interceder, Christ as indweller, Christ as ruler over the cosmos as well as head over his body, his people. Christ as the perfect exegesis of the Father, such that whoever has seen the Son has seen the Father. Christ as the first and last Word about God's divine character. Christ as the trailblazer into eternity, the model of faith and faithfulness, and as indwelling source of love, joy, peace, and also the hope of glory. The indwelling Christ now is the foretaste of glory divine. Worship must look different when these things are true. With real Christian preaching, well-grounded in both the written Word and the living Word, we learn who we are, whose we are, and how the natural life cycle of the Christian is complete in true and wholehearted worship. I would suggest that one reason worship has gone awry in recent decades is that we have lost the biblical substance in the service, including in the preaching, with a resulting spiritual amnesia about the things of greatest importance that distinguish Christian worship from any other sort. There is, of course, the loss of institutional memory that we live in an eschatological situation, where Kingdom is not simply the church; rather, we are betwixt the already of salvation coming and the not yet of salvation's completion.[2]

What, then, should eschatological worship look like if done well? Here are three pointers. First, it must be Christologically focused, must include the actual adoration of the Christ. We must not merely pray in the name of Jesus, but pray to him. This is not to suggest neglect of the Father and the Spirit, but to encourage a proper Christological emphasis and focus in our prayers, our praise, and our preaching.

Second, although eschatological worship in the twenty-first century needs to remember the past, including the past works of Christ, it must be essentially a form of forward motion, not retrograde action. We must go boldly where we have not gone before. This means new liturgies, new hymns, new praises, new forms of worship, new openness to the Spirit, and new forms of church as well as renewed focus on the teaching and preaching office of the minister. Sadly, Sunday school has been on the wane for a long time, and this means that worship has to pick up the slack and

2. See Witherington, *Imminent Domain* (Grand Rapids: Wm. B. Eerdmans, 2009).

We Have Seen His Glory

have more theological and ethical content, not less. The problem with most worship today is that it infects even willing listeners with only a *slight* case of Christianity, which prevents them from getting the real thing. We need to bear in mind once more what we learned in the first chapter of this book — in these paragraphs in particular:

> True worship is an ethical act. Indeed, it is the fulfillment of the Great Commandment to love God with all our being, and also the fulfillment of those mandates from the Ten Commandments to have no other gods and make no idols. Let me say that again: *Worship is the ultimate ethical act on earth, the most important act on earth, because it is the ultimate fulfillment of the Shema, the Great Commandment, and indeed the First and Second Commandments.*
>
> But there is a hint of something more here which has to do with things eschatological. Listen again to Jesus' words from John 4 in a more literal translation: "But the hour is coming and now is when the true/genuine worshippers will worship the Father in spirit and in truth, for the Father is seeking these sorts of worshippers. God is spirit, and for those [truly] worshipping him, it is a necessity to worship him in spirit and in truth."
>
> This, I submit, is an eschatological manifesto, a throwing down of the gauntlet. Worship can no longer be just the same old thing. Jesus is inaugurating, without fully explaining, eschatological worship, and he tells us that worshippers who worship in spirit and truth are the very sort of worshippers whom God is seeking. In fact, Jesus insists that it is necessary to worship God in spirit and truth, now that he has come and brought the Kingdom on earth.

Since real worship involves a genuine encounter with the Almighty, worship is an event, something that happens — or not. You can go to church and not worship if you experienced no meeting of the Lord in union and communion. You can be in a worship service and not worship, just like a human being can get into a swimming pool but not swim — perhaps not even know how to swim. And pastors need to be reminded that just because the mouse is in the cookie jar, it doesn't turn the mouse into a cookie! By this I mean that just because certain people are regularly in the pews doesn't mean that they are Christians or are truly worshipping.

Third, the preaching needs to be of, for, and through the text of the Bible. Needs-based preaching, or even desires-based preaching, is simply too anthropocentric. God's people often have no clue what they need from God, and their desires are so out of kilter that they are not good guides to what ought and ought not to be preached from the pulpit. If the minister will simply preach the whole counsel of God found in the Word, people's inherent needs will be ministered to, not because the worship is focused on them, but because it is focused on God — and worshippers' true needs will be met precisely by getting them to take the focus off themselves. True worship is about giving God what he desires and requires, not giving us what we want.

Fourth, it is not the job of the minister to "put the cookies on the bottom shelf." It is time to stop serving pablum in worship instead of real soul food. Instead of watering down the Gospel, we need to "boil up" the people, teasing their minds into active thought with more compelling worship and more Christ-centered preaching. The congregation needs to be challenged so that their reach will exceed their current grasp, so that they will see that they have an eschatological goal to move toward. The idea is that we are all moving collectively together toward the resurrection, and we will get there together, as the body of Christ. We will be the latter fruits of the resurrection together.

Fifth, the real issue in regard to worship is not about style — whether it is traditional or contemporary, African-American or charismatic — but about *substance*. Is God being glorified, and are the people being edified? Do God's people come anticipating a close encounter of the first kind with God? Do they come prepared to get caught up in wonder and love and praise, or do they come to critique the choir and hope for a McNugget from the preacher to take home with them?

Does worship help the congregation grow their relationship with Christ, or not? Do the people know the difference between sacrament and sacrilege, between true worship and idolatry, between a nodding acquaintance with God (caused in part by boring sermons and worship services that make them nod) and a living relationship with the Almighty? Do the people know how to identify and confess their sins to one another and receive forgiveness? Do they realize they are committed to making sure that there is no one in need among them? Do they know that it is possible to partake of the Lord's Supper — indeed, of all of worship — in an unworthy manner? Do they know that their fellow Christians are their "forever family," and so they might as well start loving them wholeheartedly, since they will be together for all eternity?

There is a reason why worship services often end with a benediction and a doxology. This is because the end and aim of all creatures great and small is doxology: the worship of the one true God. Not just any sort of worship, but worship in spirit and in truth: genuine, authentic, life-changing worship. It should all lead us into the living presence of God in Christ, where, according to the end of the Bible, we will dwell forever.

IF THIS LITTLE BOOK has teased your mind into active thought of how to do worship better in light of Kingdom come and Kingdom coming, then I am more than content. I am pleased, and I suspect so is our eschatological Alpha and Omega Lord. I can do no better than to leave you with the following reassurance:

We can expect God to provide everything necessary to make worship possible. We children of God must ever be dependent upon God, for we have no resources of our own. We are as impoverished in worship times as a baby unable to provide its own bottle at feeding time. God, the object of our worship, also becomes the inspiration of that worship. He has imparted His own Spirit into our hearts to energize that worship. All that is due Him comes from Him. His glorious Person evokes admiration for and honor of Him, as He imparts His nature into me.[3]

One more thing. If it is true that worship is what every human being created in the image of God was intended to do, and if it is true that in the End what will happen is that there will be a giant worship-fest in the Kingdom, and if it is true that the last great battle on earth will be about the hearts and minds of humankind and the nature of true worship, then it follows that worship is the most important act that anyone can do on earth. More important than acts of Congress, or acts of Parliament, or world wars — more important than anything else humans do. This being so, it would be wise for us to get on with worshipping in spirit and truth. Perhaps it is worship that God most uses not only to change individuals into his image, but to change human history and the world in which we abide. Perhaps worship is simply prayer writ large by which God shapes all things. Perhaps we need to keep singing that same old-but-new eschatological song. Does anyone know what key the Doxology is in?

Questions for Reflection and Discussion

1. Worship is different things to different people and serves many different good purposes. Draw up a list of some of these things and purposes.

---

3. Judson Cornwall, *Worship as Jesus Taught It* (Tulsa, Okla.: Victory House Publishers, 1987), p. 140.

2. Take time to write about your favorite or most meaningful worship experiences. Why were these experiences better or more memorable for you?
3. What is the communion of the saints, and how does knowing about it affect your view of worship?
4. Why do you think that worship style is so important to some Christians? Are there particular styles of worship that you find actually help you to worship? Others that hinder you? Explain why.

Bibliography

Attridge, H. "Hebrews, Epistle to the." In *The Anchor Bible Dictionary,* vol. 3, ed. D. N. Freedman, pp. 97-105. New York: Doubleday, 1992.

Burtchaell, James T. *From Synagogue to Church.* Cambridge: Cambridge University Press, 1992.

Caird, G. B. "The Exegetical Method of the Epistle to the Hebrews." *Canadian Journal of Theology* 5 (1959): 44-51.

Cameron, Averil. *Christianity and the Rhetoric of Empire.* Berkeley and Los Angeles: University of California Press, 1991.

Cornwall, Judson. *Worship as Jesus Taught It.* Tulsa, Okla.: Victory House Publishers, 1987.

Craddock, Fred. "The Letter to the Hebrews." In *The New Interpreter's Bible,* vol. 12. Nashville: Abingdon, 1998.

Davids, P. H. "The Epistle of James in Modern Debate." *ANRW* 25.5 (1988): 3622-684.

_____. "Homily, Ancient." In *Dictionary of New Testament Background,* ed. C. A. Evans and S. E. Porter, pp. 515-16. Downers Grove, Ill.: InterVarsity Press, 2000.

Dibelius, Martin. *A Commentary on the Epistle of James.* Philadelphia: Fortress Press, 1976.

Fee, Gordon. *God's Empowering Presence.* Peabody, Mass.: Hendrickson, 1994.

Gamble, Harry Y. *Books and Readers in the Early Church: A History of Early Christian Texts.* New Haven: Yale University Press, 1995.

Haines-Eitzen, K. *Guardians of Letters.* Oxford: Oxford University Press, 2000.

Harrington, D. J. *What Are They Saying about The Letter to the Hebrews?* Mahwah, N.J.: Paulist Press, 2005.

Hartin, P. J. *James and the Q Sayings of Jesus.* Sheffield: Sheffield University Press, 1991.

Helyer, L. R. *The Witnesses of Jesus, Paul, and John.* Downers Grove, Ill.: InterVarsity Press, 2008.

Hill, Craig. *Hebrews and Hellenists.* Minneapolis: Fortress Press, 1991.

Hoehner, Harold. *Ephesians: An Exegetical Commentary.* Grand Rapids: Baker, 2002.

Hughes, Graham. *Hebrews and Hermeneutics.* Cambridge: Cambridge University Press, 1979.

Jeal, Roy R. *Integrating Theology and Ethics in Ephesians.* New York: Edwin Mellen Press, 2000.

Kostenberger, A. J. "What Does It Mean to Be Filled with the Spirit? A Biblical Investigation." *JETS* 40 (1997): 229-40.

Levine, Lee. *The Ancient Synagogue: The First Thousand Years.* New Haven: Yale University Press, 2005.

_____. "The Nature and Origin of the Palestinian Synagogue Reconsidered." *Journal of Biblical Literature* 115 (1996): 425-48.

Long, Thomas. *Hebrews.* Louisville: John Knox Press, 1997.

Matera, Frank. *New Testament Theology.* Louisville: Westminster/John Knox, 2007.

Meyer, M. "The Mithras Liturgy." In *The Historical Jesus in Context,* ed. A. J. Levine, pp. 179-92. Princeton: Princeton University Press, 2006.

Murphy, F. A. "Revelation." In *Theological Interpretation of the New Testament,* ed. Kevin Vanhoozer. Grand Rapids: Baker, 2005.

Polhill, J. B. "The Life Situation of the Book of James." *Review and Expositor* 66 (1969): 369-78.

Rogers, C. L. "The Dionysian Background of Eph. 5:18." *Bibliotheca Sacra* 136, no. 1 (1979): 249-57.

Scobie, Charles H. H. *The Ways of Our God: An Approach to Biblical Theology.* Grand Rapids: Wm. B. Eerdmans, 2003.

Seid, T. W. "The Rhetorical Form of the Melchizedek/Christ Comparison in Hebrews 7." Ph.D. diss., Brown University, 1996.

Smalley, Stephen. *1, 2, 3 John.* Waco, Tex.: Word, 1984.

Trebilco, Paul. *The Early Christians in Ephesus: From Paul to Ignatius.* Tübingen: Mohr, 2004.

Vanhoozer, Kevin, ed. *Theological Interpretation of the New Testament.* Grand Rapids: Baker, 2005.

Wachob, W. H. *The Voice of Jesus in the Social Rhetoric of James.* Cambridge: Cambridge University Press, 2000.

Walters, J. "The Rhetorical Arrangement of Hebrews." *Asbury Theological Journal* 51 (1996): 59-70.

Watson, Duane. "Amplification Techniques in 1 John: The Interaction of Rhetorical Style and Invention." *Journal for the Study of the New Testament* 51 (1993): 99-123.

Wells, Sam. *Improvisation: The Drama of Christian Ethics.* Grand Rapids: Brazos Press, 2004.

Wilken, R. L. *The Christians as the Romans Saw Them.* New Haven: Yale University Press, 2003.

Witherington, Ben. *Conflict and Community in Corinth.* Grand Rapids: Wm. B. Eerdmans, 1994.

———. *The Gospel of Matthew.* Macon, Ga.: Smyth & Helwys, 2006.

———. *Imminent Domain.* Grand Rapids: Wm. B. Eerdmans, 2009.

———. *The Indelible Image,* vol. 2. Downers Grove, Ill.: InterVarsity Press, 2009.

———. *Jesus the Sage and the Pilgrimage of Wisdom.* Minneapolis: Fortress Press, 1994.

———. *Letters and Homilies for Hellenized Christians,* vol. 1. Downers Grove, Ill.: InterVarsity Press, 2006.

———. *Letters and Homilies for Jewish Christians.* Downers Grove, Ill.: InterVarsity Press, 2007.

———. *The Letters to Philemon, the Colossians, and the Ephesians.* Grand Rapids: Wm. B. Eerdmans, 2007.

———. *The Letters to the Thessalonians.* Grand Rapids: Wm. B. Eerdmans, 2005.

———. *The Living Word of God.* Waco, Tex.: Baylor University Press, 2007.

———. *Making a Meal of It: Rethinking the Theology of the Lord's Supper.* Waco, Tex.: Baylor University Press, 2007.

———. *New Testament Rhetoric.* Eugene, Ore.: Cascade Books, 2008.

———. *Troubled Waters.* Waco, Tex.: Baylor University Press, 2007.

———. *What's in the Word.* Waco, Tex.: Baylor University Press, 2009.

Wright, N. T. "Romans and the Theology of Paul." In *Pauline Theology,* vol. 3, ed. D. M. Hay et al., pp. 30-67. Minneapolis: Fortress Press, 1995.